BY LYN LIFSHIN

LYN LIFSHIN

COLD COMFORT
SELECTED POEMS 1970–1996

BLACK SPARROW PRESS SANTA ROSA 1997

ACKNOWLEDGMENTS

Thanks to the editors of the following magazines in which some of these poems have previously appeared: *ACM, American Poetry Review, The American Scholar, Aura, Bad Henry Review, Bakunnin, Black Apples, Blue Mesa Review, Brass City, Buffalo Spree, BWR, Caliban, Calyx, Caprice, Carolina Quarterly, Centennial Review, Chelsea, Chicago Review, Christian Science Monitor, Clockwatch, College English, Confrontation, Cream City Review, Denver Review, Dog River, Epoch, Farmers Market, Feminist Studies, Footwork, Free Lunch, Frontiers, George Washington Review, Georgia Review, Grain, Greensboro Review, Half Tones to Jubilee, Hammers, Hampden Sydney Review, Hawaii Review, Hiram Poetry Review, Hollins Critic, Impetus, Interim, Israel Horizons, Jeopardy, Kaimona, The Kansas Quarterly, Kiosk, Kiss the Skin Off, The Ledge, Lillabulero, Lilliput, Lillith, Lips, The Literary Review, Longshot, Lullwater Review, The MacGuffin, Mangrove, Many Mountains Moving, Medusa's Hairdo, Midwest Quarterly, Mondo Barbie, Mudfish, New Delta Review, New Digressions, New York Quarterly, North American Review, North Stone Review, Ohio Review, On the Bus, Painted Bride Quarterly, Paramour, Phoebe, Ploughshares, Portable Wall, Prairie Fire, Press, Puerto Del Sol, Rain City Review, Reed, Sellout, Seneca Review, Snail's Pace Review, Sojourner, Sonoma Mandola, The Sun, Tikkun, Upstate Madonna, Whetstone, Whiskey Island, University of Windsor Review, William and Mary Review, Witness, Wormwood Review, Yankee,* and *Yeifief.*

Black Sparrow Press books are printed on acid-free paper.

LIBRARY OF CONGRESS CATALOGING-IN-PUBLICATION DATA

Lifshin, Lyn
    Cold comfort: selected poems 1970–1996 / Lyn Lifshin
      p.   cm.
     ISBN 1-57423-040-9 (pbk. : alk. paper). — ISBN 1-57423-041-7 (cloth trade : alk. paper). — ISBN 1-57423-042-5 (signed cloth : alk. paper).
     I. Title.
PS3562.I4537C65   1997
811'.54—dc21

97-26949
CIP

TABLE OF CONTENTS

BIOGRAPHY

MOTHERS, DAUGHTERS

OTHER PEOPLE

OTHER PLACES

COLD COMFORT

SELECTED POEMS 1970–1996

BIOGRAPHY

ONYXVELVET
(AUTOBIOGRAPHY)

You Know the Story

of the woman in a
turret and how ivy
puts its fingers
across the moon.
And besides, no one
could hear. Ivy
that grows forever
against the dankest
part of a wall,
gnawing gargoyles
deep in the belly
of the house. I would
have lowered my hair
to a lover, lured
him with blood
in a bottle, each
drop a ruby with
a poem etched on it.
Or carved my initials
in the grey stone
around my heart.
I'd have talked to
the birds or waited,
slept twenty years,
given away my children.
Only I was outside,
trying to get in

Dream of the Pink and Black Lace, Just like the Evening Gown

my favorite in high school,
a dress I'd waited to see
marked down and finally wrote
the store, even then, able
to get what I wanted

more easily on paper. I
told them how often I'd come
back, hoping it would be marked
down and dashed up with my
mother when they agreed
to lower the price.

I feel the swirl of those
gowns I ran my hand through,
terrified mine wouldn't
be there, then carrying it as
carefully as a baby of blown glass.

It was so full my waist
looked tiny inside it
with hoops and an eyelet bustier.
The dress took up half
my mother's closet,

less space than I did in her,
especially after she had me.
I don't think I wore it again, too
dressy, too much lace to pack.
But I can see it near the yellow

16

and the pink and white gauzy gowns,
swirling strapless, a part of 38
Main Street I expected to always
be as it was, like my mother,
waiting for me to fill it

FAT

Some of it I've
given away, I guess that
comes from thinking
nobody could
want it.
Fat. Something you
take in and just
can't use.
It hangs around
reminding you of what
wasn't totally
digested, a layer of heavy
water, grease

having so
much I'd dream the
4:30 tall thin
shadow thighs were
me, pressed so hard it
hurt, a
punishment squeezing
myself into
me, into
what I didn't
want. Afternoons
with the shades drawn
examining and hating what
I saw, longing for one of those
svelte bodies

I put the
scales back, would have

beat myself with
rubber chains

when I was 12 I bought a
rubber girdle, nobody
knew I peeled it off with the
door locked

Somebody once said
you'll never get
cold this winter
fat legs
like that

How could something like fat ever
protect you from anything
outside being only an
extension of yourself, cells
spreading, making you
more vulnerable,
fat people having more
places to bruise
or scar

I sat in a room and
watched the
river when
other girls
were going across the
state line,
were necking in cars at
Lake Bomoseen
despising those
layers I
didn't need

belly that
I hated and squeezed into
clothes a size
too small, hips, but
worse, thighs I
hated them
most, spreading out
on benches
for basketball practice

Once I lay on my
back cycling air until
the room spun

white waves of the body
I was so ashamed I wouldn't go
to the beach

my mother always
said *Yes, you're pretty
eat* and I curled
into myself
eating what made
me worse

tho I wanted to
wear pleats
and be delicate

In one store a
man asked her
*is it difficult
having one daughter
who's so lovely?* and I
hated my sister for being
blond, her body

like a Keene
waif, I was jealous of
her eggnogs and
chocolate
how meat had to be
coaxed to her
bones

You can't camouflage
hold anything in
that long, it explodes
a rubber girdle pops
elastic
letting go
then they know
that there's more
than you can
handle.

look at me now and
you say *but those
thin wrists*

Listen when I weigh
over a hundred I
break out in
hives. We

all think of our
selves the way
we were

especially when it
comes to what we
don't love

Once when I was
walking home from
school the elastic
on my underpants died
The next day someone
wrote kike on the
blackboard
Both I knew were a result
of fat

I've never been good
at getting rid of
what I can't use
but that's when I
knew that I had to

that round face with
glasses, bulging
thighs. You know

when some man says
love it's still
hard to believe

If I wear my clothes
too short, it's to
remind myself (I still
avoid mirrors,
glass) that my

legs are not
unlovable, I

want you to see I finally am
someone you might
want to dance with

this me waiting under
neath on the
sidelines

years of
getting down to

But it really is
sweetest close
to the bone

HAIR

In Brooklyn one
love's aunt plotted
made an appointment
to have it done
cut in a flip

a present for me
like the scratchy
nylon gowns I
never wore when I
left to marry

an uncle said before
he died he wished
he could see it
short. After

the wedding I
pulled pins out of
that stiff hive
for a week, afraid
to touch it

when I taught in
highschool I had
to wear it up
sprayed it one
grey morning
with flit as

if it was a
living flying

thing that
shouldn't, like
my life seemed
that October

unreal, I was
afraid to touch
it, all his family
tried to pull it
back into velvet

twist it, pin
it choke, they said
they wanted to see
my eyes but I
know they suspected
me of being a
hippie, a witch

the college that
said I couldn't stay
on white cold paper
wrote first can't you look more
professional and

dignified, wear
it up. The brother
in law would pull
it, sneer, ask if I'd
seen the mad

hair girl in
The Munsters. I
heard that the whole tv season.
Later I learned that

what grew out of
the dark where I
couldn't reach
like dreams or
poems was beautiful

shouldn't be
squeezed into
changed into
something different

but those years
apologizing, stuffing
the sun bleached red
under my collar

straightening it
and never letting it
go where it wanted

milkweed, wild
flowers, poems animals

a dream, hair
like someone who
couldn't, hadn't
wouldn't admit, didn't
know it had a
life of its own

BLUE VELVET PILLOWS

Now, with most of the
stuffing gone. In the
early fifties, the
grey cat peed on them.
Pillows that our baby
sitter, Lela, propped
me against, asked did I
want to play doctor, put
her tongue in and then
wanted me to stick my head in
her big bush. Blue velvet,
color of spilled ink, of
midnight Vermont blues,
waiting for David to call.
Blue velvet, my mother
would curl at one end of, me
at another as my father's
hair made a print on the
gold chair where he never
said anything. I'd prop
blue velvet high up for
dates and curl with my shoes
off in the dark, waiting for
the closed dining room door to
open. Velvet the color of Liz
Taylor's eyes covered with
Christmas paper after we no
longer hid the tree in the
closet, hearing Gramp come
up stairs. Not scratchy but
soft as a cat. My face in the
blue. I could hear wind from

Otter Creek. In the street
below people were laughing.
50 generations of cats could
have dozed in this blue, the
pillows as thin as a blue woman,
used, flattened out, a blue
mysterious as those all night
blues you can't let go of

YELLOW ROSES

pinned on stiff tulle,
glowed in the painted
high school moonlight.
Mario Lanza's *Oh My
Love.* When Doug
dipped I smelled
Clearasil. Hours in
the tub dreaming of
Dick Wood's fingers
cutting in, sweeping
me close. I wouldn't
care if the stuck
pin on the roses
went thru me,
the yellow musk
would be a wreathe
on the grave of that
awful dance where
Louise and I sat
pretending we didn't
care, our socks fat
with bells and fuzzy
ribbons, silly as we
felt. I wanted to be
home, wanted the
locked bathroom to
cry in, knew some
part of me would
never stop waiting
to be asked to dance

WRITING CLASS, SYRACUSE WINTER

Write, he said looking
like an even craggier
Lincoln, *your impressions,*
the next four days, details
of a walk across campus.
Even now I remember I
wore a strawberry wool
skirt, matching sweater.
There was bittersweet
near the Hall of Language.
I curled in a window
ledge of a cave in Crouse,
an organ drifting thru
smooth warm wood. I
could let the wine
dark light hold me, slid
on the ice behind where
a man with a blue mole
picked me up, my notes
scattering up Comstock.
I was hypnotized by that
huge growth, said yes
tho I only half remembered.
Upstairs, icicles clotted,
wrapped glass in gauze.
There must have been some
one who didn't call. Blue
walls, ugly green bedspread.
Dorothy popping gum, eating
half a tuna sandwich before
we'd lie in bed with the
lights out wondering what

it would be like to have
Dr. Fox with his red beard
go down on us as we
braided and rubbed our
mahogany hair dry and I
tried to figure out what to
do with the bittersweet,
ragged maples, didn't
believe I'd ever have any
thing to write about

MAMA

I read *Love With
Out Fear* on the
toilet I'm 8 I hear
them fighting no
is a tight bracelet
closes my legs to
gether near the
Episcopal Church
where Doug's lips
brush my hot

if a girl lets a
man put his tongue
in her teeth she'll
let him do any
thing, page seven
teen drifts up out
of that bathroom
thru the chest
nuts, no taped on
my camp clothes
on the crotch of
jeans so tight
I can't button
them, it was

in my bed all
that marriage, no
it hurts the nut
meg makes me
dizzy no I can't
who's heard of

living in the
trees with a
wanted poet no
David I can't go
California no
Fatimi the white
slave market the
Arab leaves the no

Paul I wouldn't in
the lilacs, Mama
don't always keep
talking of how
people are talking
I'm not 15 and
won't don't worry
that the man with
a hat won't want
to marry, has a wife

For years I
couldn't leave the
man who wouldn't
let me dance and
laughed at my
singing, you
wonder what kind
of a woman sleeps
around, rum in
her pocketbook,
salve. The first
time I said yes
was in a locked
room on paper

Yes I would to
the man in another
town but what if
I'm frigid. How
could he tell
listen this is
not so bad Mama
don't worry about
the man with super
dope on his lips

he wants to kiss
my eyes my ass shove
no out of me with
his you know what
Mama, it's ok love Lyn

You Understand the Requirements

We are
sorry to have to
regret to
tell you
sorry sorry
regret sorry that you have
failed

your hair should have been
piled up higher

you have failed to
pass failed
your sorry
regret your
final hair comprehensive
exam satisfactorily
you understand the requirements

you understand we are
sorry final

and didn't look professional
as desirable
or sorry dignified
and have little enough
sympathy for 16th century
sorry English Anglicanism

we don't know doctoral
competency what to think and
regret you will sorry not

be able to stay
or finish

final regret your disappointment
the unsuccessfully completed best
wishes for the future
it has been a
regret sorry the requirements
the university policy

please don't call us

ORALS

Half of them
cough, the one
with the limp wittily
grunts towards me
you remind me of
Theda Bara, a distant
relative I blush be
cause it's true.
Already
his eyes are
full of no.
Smoke boils up from the
table, the scraped faces
freeze on me until I
wish I hadn't come

suddenly this glass voice
clangs and what do you
think of adultery. Now
it is not easy to be
clever under his
fluorescent glare but
I look right back and
ask how that's
relevant, he doesn't
like that at all

scratches an ear and wants
to know if Tottel's 3rd
cousin by a later
marriage of course
is significant in 19th

century bibliography and
my God he is serious I
sweat inside my specially
lengthened drab grey suit

beginning to think of
oceans, imagining that
walls could drift
out slowly, even
the floor slide away,
not able to suppose
just then why Marvell
didn't write the
same poems that Donne
did briefly in 72
seconds, or where
Fulke Greville was
while Spenser was
having his fire

the two faces I thought
I knew keep dissolving
their eyes float to
shelves where words
live predictably

are you certain of
those dates a British
accent whines thru
teeth that have never
lived outside New
York City. A stranger
bends into his shoes
as if the laces were
nastily disappointing

We know your record
the Milton man spits
thru a belch but you
understand the require
ments, couldn't you
just have a baby

THE PEARLS

An engagement present, from my husband's parents.
Shoved in a drawer like small eggs waiting to hatch,
forgotten. They seemed like something in a high school
photograph. I'd have preferred a large wrought iron
   pendant,
beads that caught the sun. Pearls were for *them*

and I was always only a visitor, tho he said he wished
I'd call him Dad. Sam was all I could get out,
it was hard to throw my arms around him, to bubble
and kiss. And not just because they thought
me a hippie, a witch, thought I took

their son's car and stamps and coin collections.
Pearls wouldn't go with my corduroy smocks, long black
ironed hair. They didn't blend with my hoops of onyx
and abalone that made holes in my ears but caught the
   light.
Pearls might have gone with the suits I threw away,

no longer a graduate student trying to please.
They weren't suitable for days with a poet hidden in trees
or for throwing up wine in toilet bowls after poetry readings
where I shook and swore not to let anyone see. My spider
   medallion
is in at least eight poems. Pearls remind me of the way I
   thought

I was: studious but not wild, not interesting. But I put
   those pearls
on last night tho I hadn't planned to wear them. They didn't
   seem ugly

40

or apt to choke, seemed gentle and mild as so little is in my
    life
these days. I slept in nothing but those pearls, they seemed
part of me

scraps, the handwriting
that had sloped in the
yellow light of Florence
toward where each line
was heading, now almost
too real with its "this
is impossible" under a
line from the man sing-
ing near Rue de la Harpe
moaning where do I go
from here. I said I
didn't know how to
change anything. How
little I knew. And then
the spit out, leaning
backward like trees
squashed toward the
left by monsoon winds,
"I feel dead, dead,"
darkly underlined

DRIFTING

things I have and
don't have
come from this
moving between
people like leaves like
smoke. I've been
waiting the way
milkweed I
brought inside two
years ago stays
suspended, hair in the
wind it seems to
float, even its
black seeds don't
pull it down
tho you don't under
stand how any
thing could stay
that way
so long

AFTER DARK MY SWEET
(LOVE AND EROTICA)

Why Aerograms Are Always Blue

Because of the distance to you
because the wind fades,
dries out the verbs
until the background they've
leaned against blends
with the sky.
The blue reflects your eyes.
No, that's a lie, I don't
remember them, only the
feeling in my hands, some
thing longing, aching the
blue in my veins a fast
blue burning barriers

NOT QUITE SPRING

Baby you know I get high
on you, come back with me
whispering in her ear
it was all she could do to say
no, spring leaves budding
his hand on her breast
crocus smell and
everything unfolding
she gasping I want, I
would but instead hurrying
back to the windowless room
where she locks the heavy door.
Lemons are rotting on her pillow,
she studies her nipples,
nyloned crotch in mirror
then hugs her huge body to sleep

FITZI IN THE YEARBOOK

grin muffled but
sneaky, slithering
out like his penis
did in the Drive in
a June before I could
imagine anything so
slippery sliding up,
let alone inside
me after months of
Saturdays in my
mother's grey apartment
my sister Joy giggling
behind the couch,
a tongue pressing between
lips should have been
a warning in the
blue Chevy I felt
he was all whale
crashing with his
"now you've done
this to me, you have
to," everything in
me sand he
collapsed on

Tentacles, Leaves

He saw my
picture in a
magazine and told
me he wanted
to take me down
the Mississippi
hollering poems and
blowing weed, he
sounded crazy
and I wrote that I'd
never been
beaten that I was
a bitch

he sent me
pain and lust
for 19 days his
aloneness, how he
wanted to fall
into blue water
he said my letters
fell apart
pressed to his
skin. In March
my arms started
melting and

I drank the
Château Ausone
he sent, by April
my face was
burning, he sent

me his so that in
Concord I could
just think about
him while the
river was
swelling

but I didn't
think he'd
come, writing bad
checks, stealing
hamburg staggering
with a torn
suitcase and broken
shoes from California
I didn't know where
to keep him

and I got drunk on
cognac before he
fell thru the
door

he taught me
what men did in
prison his

eyes weren't mean
and blue
when he said how
we would live in a
house of shells in
the ferns in
Big Sur
high on poems

he said we'd eat the
colors off Point
Lobos, dark
wine and succulents in
bed. I could
hear the
seals afternoons
we lay in a blur
of nutmeg
watching the curtains

his head on my
belly telling me about
women who
stopped mattering

that's when it
started getting
scary one
waited five years after
getting a short
letter

I wouldn't even
take the bus
across town
tho I dreamed I'd go
with him
to Yugoslavia
and Mexico

he kept getting busted
and moved under the
stairs with
dead moths

drinking beer
and not coughing
then he moved
out into
the trees

came leaf by
leaf in the morning

fog was what we
needed, a blur to
lie down and
lie in. I
never liked his
poems as
much as I
pretended, not
even the ones
he stole

but I loved the
stories, how he
made love in
coffins, stood
on the roof of his
house screaming
at stars
But he kept
breaking into
places. Once
I held him
4 hours while
he cried

next morning he

poured chocolate
on my lips
and ate it and
talked about
going to Montana

we could live in a
wooden hut in
Canada with my cats

only nothing was
getting better
he vomited blood
and black things
if he came in
late I thought
it was over

he'd just laugh
we'd take a bottle
out into the
huge weeds
and collapse
laughing

other things fell
too, leaves
he'd slam into
chairs with
cigarettes, burn
holes in everything

I set the clock
ahead, wondered
how long this could
go on, the snow

coming and I
watered the mail
when he went to
get better

and didn't
by October I
couldn't move

wherever I went
there were
tentacles, his
eyes in the
window

I tripped on his
arms and then
cut out for Colorado

he couldn't just
stay in the
leaves, children
said he smelled
like fire

lady bugs lie on
their backs now the
wind is rising

I'm not
sorry that he
came

or that nothing
could keep him

maybe
it could have
been because of
rain that we fell
together so
easily that first time
rain keeping the
others near the
fire your hair was
blacker than the melon
seeds under the straw the towels
smelling of sweet trees our
bodies lifted to each other in the
rain cottage the
wet leaves pulling us
close and down

ALL AFTERNOON WE

read Lorca
by five snow
blurred the
glass, February, I
leaned against
those chill panes
gypsies
burned through the
snow with apples
You in the
other room
I was thinking
don't let
this be some
warmth I can
move near
and never know

Lemon Wind

All day
nobody wanted
to talk

the sleeping bags
were still wet
from the storm
in Cholla Vista

Nothing went right.

But later the
wood we
burned had a sweet
unfamiliar sweet

and all night
we could taste
lemons in the wind

NOT THINKING IT WAS SO WITH YELLOW FLOWERS

At night I
dreamed that
same dream,
the one
full of muscles
and thighs
that aren't you.
Later the fear
came back
crossing into
Mexico tho
at first
when I woke up
I thought it
wasn't true
the air was so
bright and
yellow flowers
were falling
from the
pepper tree
like suns

Even There

it was December
and yes finally
you wanted me
we ran down the
slick narrow road
houses leaned
together the colors
wine and brown
remember the cracked
snow our scarves
floating getting
there out of
breath our
hair melting
boots clicked under
the door there
were quilts on the
sloped ceiling
and the old
stove you smiled
toward going to
heat up some
coffee. I kept
looking around
to get it right:
your suede jacket
hanging in several
places your
mouth was
corduroy I wanted
to touch
but even in the

dream every
time I came
close to you
the place that
was you
changed to air

LUST BLOWING UNDER THE DOOR, BRIGHT AS STRAW

Your smile's like sun
flowers he said
as tho
embarrassed his
hands were
pressing awkwardly the
ring on his
second finger
close to her
eyes
from that room
a wheat sea
lust blew under the
door bright
as straw
and his warm
parts on
her belly
those small
bones that changed her
small
bones to water
And not even
knowing
his name
until later
when the floor fell
the room
turned into a
painting
and the paint cracked

MUSTACHE

I was thinking
of it this
morning, those
marvelous hairs that
curl around your words

and how they smelled with
frost all over
in the mountains

And yes especially of that
time on the floor
looking like the
middle part of a thick
leggy bug I could

just see
above my belly, moist and
floating up
asked

is this
making your blood glow

WEEDS AND WOODSMOKE

your tattoo that
one gold earring

how your red beard
was only red in
places. Love,
your strong tongue

pieces of a night
coming back like
petals in the only
kind of flower
I can draw

wild, bright
not connected
to any center

ON THE NEW ROAD

red sumac presses
against the windshield,
tires moan

Your wife dreams
you are guilty

I button and unbutton
what I feel

NOVEMBER 1 BOOGIE

on the third floor
rug rolled back
shoes under the sofa
toes instead of words
hair swinging like
Spanish moss in
to a slow blues
kelp tangling in
water that shakes
hips and lips free
skin making love to
a whole room. No
wonder the Shakers
danced till they
couldn't stand
went home with
grass stains,
starved

RIVERWIND, MAGNOLIAS

How we could hear
the slap of water
lights on the Mohawk
the way you can almost
see the color of a
tulip in rain
before it is
Let's you said *do you*
want to, we
could walk
down by the river
Lips of wine, I was
pulled the
magnolias opening
apricot river
warm leather and the
water smells. Lilac
wind. My lips
so open
you pulled me
down toward the bench,
pulled my hand
to where you
were least shy

WITH YOUR NAME LEAKING DOWN MY SKIN

Baby, you know it's because
of you my hair won't
stop moaning, that you've
got everything that makes
my blood reach out for you
thru these cracked greasy
nights. And I know you
used to care so why (I
heard you still have that
crooked mustache, dark
ruby lies) won't you at
least pretend to want to
want me? My nipples are
lonely, my beads drip your
name and I shouldn't have
told you to go. Come on
back, the way your name
leaks down my skin, well
it's gonna drown me

NAMES

Lately I become
whatever you call
me, the way some
Indians do. First
I couldn't say
yours because
it belonged to
someone who'd
turned me into
who I wasn't.
When you called
me *love* near the
rag shop on Caroline,
I tried to remember
the spell Iroquois
put on names to
make them stay

Having You Come Up after So Much Time

thinking what it
would be like re-
reading your letter
like a map I folded
September then un-
folded it again. I
thought I was
ready but it was
like thunder you
hear on the phone
when you're talking
to someone where
the storm is. You
know it's coming
moving east like
most weather but
you still wake up
startled, dazed.
When it breaks, the
rain on the glass,
the lightning that
makes the room
even darker

READING THOSE POEMS BECAUSE I CAN'T GET STARTED THINKING OF THE PHONE CALL THAT CAME, THAT YOU MIGHT

before I get to the
end of the line, my
head's milkweed.
Something in me
drifts out into the
trees thru the
stained glass, my
black seeds flying
out to where you
say we'll find
columbine. They
get hung up in the
leaves, words sinking
in where they can't
grow like what
was starting to
in the shot deer
left in the
snow all winter

After a Day We Stay in Bed until the Sun Is Close to Setting

He drives home
thru the black trees
with a poem
about me that will
make him famous
starting in his
fingers. He wishes
the wheel was his
Olympia typewriter.
He needs to get my
hair where he can
touch it on the long
drive thru the pine
trees, my musk still
drenching the car.
I want to read
this poem almost as
much, dazed, the
night's performance
has sucked me flat
and pale as an empty
sheet of non erasable
bond, has pulled
all color, all the
wet moist verbs
out the way he took
the stories I told
and made them in
to his own surreal
dreams. Even my
leaves and branches

became the green
arms of a child
My mouth is dry, I
need to have his
poem where my clove
nipples press into his
blue stripped cotton
smelling of sun and
wind in the pine
trees, a mirror that
will reflect my dark
eyes. I need this as
much as he needs
to invent me to
become himself

LOVE LIKE SHOPLIFTING

A challenge,
silver dollars on
the railroad track
with the train
coming, flashing
light up in
the leaves. Love,
you could be
the Jack of Hearts,
something I don't
need, probably
won't use but
start, like dropping
the priceless sword
into stretched out
nylon bikinis and
walking to the
door as if metal
wasn't rubbing
the lips under that
hair. A game, six
pair of velvet pants
crushed into
boots under my
skin tight straight
skirt slit to
my knees that I'm
walking casually in as if
there were years to
get past the door
before zippers burst like
spit balls, grenades

and what's inside slams out
like fat or tears
giving what's
what away

THE CHILD WE WILL NOT HAVE

Will be a boy. Dean Michael
will go to law school and play
football. I'll listen to September
get loud and then quieter,
sneak into the smallest room

to write s.o.s. notes in returnable soda
bottles, my belly crinkled as the toe nail
that falls off after a torturous summer
of pointe. This child you always wanted
swims in my arms like that gone nail,

I talk to it with my mouth shut. It teaches
you to sign, lip reads my nipples. In the movie
of September, some of the stills are missing.
I clutch the baby like someone at a crash site,

hear glass fall. The child we will not have
is all we wanted, all that holds us together

HE SAID IN THE HOSPITAL IT

isn't much like
you'd imagine
they're joking
paraplegics putting
on rock n roll real
loud to bug some dudes
who just like Aida
We were glad to be
coming out of the jungle,
not in body bags.
First day out with my
new leg and I think I'm
hot stuff, don't know its
got this spring-loaded
thing and I twist on
a bar stool and my
leg spits and flings
itself out, yanks a
brief case off this
man's arm and throws it
across the floor. He
gives me a funny look.
Then once one foot
turned around so
I looked to be
walking backward and
forward and a kid
pointed it out
and said look at that
man as his mama was
hushing. You'd be
surprised what I can

do with it. But,
Honey, there are
some things it's more
comfortable to
take it off for

AFTERNOONS IN THE BLUE RAIN

When I still wondered
if you'd call. Now
those Junes, a cake
of soap made out of
flesh, a lampshade you
can see where a
nipple or tendon
was. I'll wait
in the dark for the
ice you left plunged
in me like a mugger's
knife to melt into
the Hudson River. First
I thought your heart was
in your penis. Now I
can see it was in
the leg you saw
torn from you
on the other side of the
road, Vietnam

NICE

floating thru chairs
then opening
your hand
snakes in thru corduroy
my slip rides up the sun
makes the rug into a wool beach
sand, assapples, a wave of
thighs opening
skin prints a v on the rug your
knees go there
opening
and mouths suddenly too a
crack touch the pink smell
the sleek breathing flesh moans
a taste is nipples
bumping and your sail of blood
shove of bone tongue
travelling into this moist
lips opening the first bang of
hair and clothes rise from bodies
tremble the warm buttons rubbing
scratch of your mouth there
the damp nylon crotch
petals dissolving in a water my silk
hips you open and your fingers
under plunge so are pressing lips there
and your flesh
roots shining
rocks your heat to my belly and my
legs spread so wide
greedy for the whole boat of you
in me your lovejuice dipping these

sloppy hills of cunt and you
put your good
hardness up me opening
skin rooms pounding
and circles slide your raw stem
my nails pull you
tighter
in and the slap of licked flesh oil
waves lunging and teeth
that eat everywhere ramming
the slit wet
opening and spread so
wide and splitting bite the sweet hot ache swell
your bomb breaking
too sucks the whole room up
fur zippersbeercans
and the sweat hair of groaning and sperm
till your cock bud throbs more
to ball me over and
again, better than summer
deep and nice
bringing everything
home

WHIPS AT THE RITZ

He said he remembered
how her hair caught
on the hotel's silver
foil, on chocolate.
It was before Godiva
but tasted better
when she rubbed
some down there for
him to lick off.
He could still taste
the rose of her
chained open legs,
chocolate cherries
stained sheet he
couldn't have resisted.
Serena just grinned.
The whips stunned him
on the floor as if
begging or praying,
the smell of the rug.
It was harder than
he said to lose weight,
harder to resist such
sweets than to pass
any of his orals
at Harvard, addictive,
dangerous he moaned
but magical as seeing
Christ or birth

WITH SO MANY VOICES

The play switches so fast
I couldn't remember
what part I was cast
in, your words, like a lid
over my eye so I had
to feel where I was
going, learning which
tone curled like a lip,
like a polaroid in a
hot damp room rain
leaks in. I moved by
touch, could have been
blind folded on a velvet
couch with no panties
on, legs on silk pillows
gilt chains spiralled
from, being entered
by strangers, my dark
parts throbbing like
a throat exploding
in a rash of roses

YOUR WORDS

hammers between
the veal calves
eyes, the
red stain. Head
less chickens
stagger in wet
grass where
a child will
dream about
them twisting
in a night sweat,
running to a
mother's arms
in the moon
who sees her
father sitting
on her glitter-
ing like the knife

In This Version

she keeps him on
ice, like an
illegal pistol
in a safe
deposit box,
to finger and
cock and then
wrap back
in soft flannel.
He's there
for her, ready
for her fingers.
She moves closer,
strokes his pearl
handle, Bonnies
up to his
Clyde, tongues
his cross hairs.
He's cool, he's
hard, ready
for her to,
with just the
touch of her
skin, explode,
leave only a
white puff, the
scent of him
on her skin

SOMEWHERE IN THE MIDWEST

A man can almost hear
the wind cracking
frozen cornstalks.
When he lets the cat

in, cold glows around
the silver fur like
those rings around the
moon that mean some

thing's happening.
He hums a blues tune
in a cold room full
of paper. This could

be Madison or maybe
Red Granite. He
could remember a
woman he held one

night with hair
longer and blacker
than it was. If
he decides she's just

a travelling lady
he puts down the
phone, listens
to branches, doesn't

write what he feels
in a room as cold

as hers where she
hears frost etch

the moon out too

WITH YOU

it wasn't like trying
to ride a wild roan,
forcing my legs to
bend to the shape
of a strange body,
but more like going
out to just touch
the old mare under
a blood moon, the
grass turning brittle
past yellowing
brush the stone
wall still hugs.
The last ruby light
still warms your
own fingers until the
mare nuzzles them.
She expects the
apple, knows the
shape of your
nails as I've rolled against
the mare and hooves
of you, dreaming
a book with
fewer surprises,
less chance to
be flung down
or into wire

AFTERWARD

There was the sense of
someone who'd driven
dogs thru the darkest
strands of Alaska
making it alone.
The snow could have
been my body
opened up, a white
to get thru in
the night burnt
tracks thru his
heart beat as
sweat dripped, left
his blue sweater
soaking. He pressed
past, heart in
tact, alone with
the road in snow
my smell vanishing
as he yelps commands
to the dogs on the
way to remember
what he'd leave fast
enough to long for

INDIAN SUMMER

after the too early
October snow bending
trees to splitting
after I wrapped
in blackness
alone, no lights
no hot water
your voice, a
light on the radio
batteries are losing
whatever they had
after phones stopped
then started, without
your voice, your voice
in my room, rivers
in my dream
melting as my
thighs would in
your blue bed as
long as November
stayed swollen with
light until in
hours it would be
come a bell with
its tongue cut out

SNOW FENCES, WORMWOOD

in your room of
sun and metal

ghosts of indians
the barns crumbling

wormwood inside us
only we didn't know

saw only the ice
cones dripping the

sheet's tangle smelling
good you said

as a woman had been there

Shadows of Steam on Champagne, Concrete

Some say when someone
blind from birth
gets sight back
shadows are puzzling
as ghosts, a twin
distorted, stain that
moves along with you,
mimics, a dark
shape leaning from
light. I've felt as
dogged by dreams
there and then, not.
Licorice forms like
but not exactly
what I knew, a
litany of mystery
that dissolves
quicker the way when
a lover leaves the
sun of his eyes
still turns my
skin rose, more
like a rash I'll
see in harsher
light when all I
wanted was for our
shapes, like a
plane merging
with its shadow
to merge safely

OTHER SEPTEMBERS

wrapping the green tomatoes
on the first night the cold
was tangible
as a cloth, it

took all the cats
tangled in tomato vines
before we could go
up stairs, put

wood on the stove
Skin smelled of that
green, grasshoppers in
the moon like small

black lights. It
would take weeks of
snow with green
tomatoes frying in

side and the windows
foggy to know there
was nothing of
summer left

living. Nights were
frozen reeds.
You and I were
like a river running

toward what we
didn't know

Leaving Rome

olive branches slap
chrome, the sky's a
blue clearer than
agates. Cobblestones,
arches balanced as
precariously as our
words in the car
as if we both knew
something besides
the trip was ending
tho lulled in the
over grown amphi-
theater where rose
light licked our
skin and turned
hair mahogany.
Frascati helped
make the black
glow tho stones in
us were falling
like those in the
basilica at Saint
Sebastian and we
were scratched,
dug into and dark
as the catacombs
where frescoes
peal and those
waiting for the
Nazis huddled,
clinging to stones

LIGHT FROM THIS TURNING

I have lost touch with
distant trees,
the wind you brought
in your hair
and lilac hills.

Something different
bites into the river
and the river of lost days
floats over my tongue.

Love, you are like that
distant water, pulling
and twisting,
you turn me

apart from myself
like some frightening road,
something I don't want
to know.

Still, let my
hair float slow through
this new color,
let my eyes absorb
all light

from this turning
that has brought us
here, has carried us
to where we are
we are

93

DESPITE EVERYTHING
(FAMILY)

There Were Blue Grapes behind the House

Grey painted wide boards
bugs could sleep in.
Wasps slivered through
screens on 38 Main St
and the lilac room
was 24 shades of plum.
The sun's tongue only
went so far. Shards.
Rooms. Pieces. Stuck
to each other like
the glass in teapots
glazed with hair line
cracks, like a fat
woman held tight in
nylon so she seems
somebody else. Freeze
frames like slices
of music, some Bach,
a little old black
jazz, music from the
stone ages up to
punk on that ninety
minute cassette
packed into Voyager
on its trip with no
known end through
the stars

SOMEWHERE NEAR VILNA

Past where the train
goes where snow
mounds in the shape
of caves and ovens,
my father is holding
one hand near an
eye, tracing the
sun's rouge light
in snow. Later no
one will be sure
why he can't see,
moves thru shadows
with just his left
eye. A chicken
that will bleed
over straw by
noon the next
day, nests near the
foot of the bed
his mother made
of evergreen and
patched wood. Cold
spreads like oil
or terror. An aunt
talks of the year
there was no thaw,
her skin cracked,
rough as a cat's
tongue, reads to
my father in candle
light of a country
with no snow where,

if my father can
learn to read
symbols he doesn't
know, rooms of silver
warm as a cow's belly
will open to him

MY FATHER TELLS US ABOUT LEAVING VILNIUS

On the night we left Vilnius, I had to bring goats
next door in the moon. Since I was not the youngest, I
couldn't wait pressed under a shawl of coarse cotton
close to Mama's breast as she whispered "hurry" in Yiddish.
Her ankles were swollen from ten babies. Though she was
only thirty her waist was thick, her lank hair hung in

strings under the babushka she swore she would burn
in New York City. She dreamt others pointed and snickered
near the tenement, that a neighbor borrowed the only bowl
she brought that was her mother's and broke it. That night
every move had to be secret. In rooms there was no heat in,
no one put on muddy shoes or talked. It was forbidden to
    leave,

a law we broke like the skin of ice on pails of milk. Years
    from
then, a daughter would write that I didn't have a word for
America yet, that night of a new moon. Mother pressed my
brother to her, warned everyone even the babies must not
    make
a sound. Frozen branches creaked. I shivered at men with
guns near straw roofs on fire. It took our old samovar, every

coin to bribe someone to take us to the train. "Pretend to be
sleeping," father whispered as the conductor moved near.
    Mother
stuffed cotton in the baby's mouth. She held the mortar and
pestle wrapped in my quilt of feathers closer, told me I
    would
sleep in this soft blue in the years ahead. But that night I
was knocked sideways into the ribs of the boat so sea sick I

couldn't swallow the orange someone threw from an upstairs
bunk tho it was bright as sun and smelled of a new country I
could only imagine though never how my mother would
    become
a stranger to herself there, forget why we risked dogs
and guns to come

I Was Four, in Dotted

Swiss summer pajamas,
my face a blotch of
measles in the small
dark room over the blue
grapes and rhubarb,
hot stucco cracking
17 North Seminary
that July Friday
noon my mother was
rushed in the grey
blimp of a Chevy
north to where my
sister Joy would be
born two months
early. I wasn't
ready either and
missed my mother's
cool hands, her
bringing me frosty
glasses of pineapple
juice and cherries
with a glass straw
as Nanny lost her
false teeth, flushed
them down the toilet
then held me so tight
I could smell lavender
and garlic in her
braided hair, held
me as few ever
have since, as if
not to lose more

ESTELLE, STAR STONES

That summer on the sea porch, Winthrop, was
it July? My sister crying. Estelle,
even your name a bracelet, star stones

stars I put on and let my sister
touch to stop, let the dark waves crash
on the bed. We were drifting into your 19 year
old life, imagining your boyfriends on the
other edge of your skin. Nipples on the beach, your

tan. You brought blue bowls of raspberries,
cream fingers. Estelle, Estelle, you wanted
to be what your name was and sang weekends on
the radio, sang brushing my hair in the
bathroom light. The white tiles cool.
My sun burnt skin. You said

you'd never stop singing, wouldn't marry and
hummed something that both our fathers heard
on that boat from Lithuania, heard in a
strange tongue. We couldn't understand
you said but would later and how
you'd dance as those children
had. Black pines.

Russia glowing in the sea. Night. We were
wrapped in cats and velvet. Moon on
the stones. You told us of dreams hidden
in the stone, got out that—I remember
the gold around the latch—

jewel box, it was what went with wishes

in old books and moonstones. Dream
fur. Choose one for later.

The smoothest stones. Your long thick hair.
Goodnight. Your name a charm still
though you married in some split level,
your throat stuffed with china
and none of the things you
promised would happen happened

New England Sunday

Main street was empty
except for clots of cars
near the Episcopal Church
where dark stone grew moss
on the north side and
boys threw pennies
down into the rail
road tracks.

I pressed against glass,
wished I had to put on a
skirt with a half slip
to sit in the cool stained glass,
my hair brushed then
braided, never as straight
as I wanted it.

Later the rooms would be
hot, the blood light
sinking, turning my
lavender walls mauve,
orchid, raspberry. We'd
come back from Branbury
Beach or my grand
mother's porch
half asleep. I was
already too heavy
to be carried.

Lulled by grownups'
slap of cards on the
screened porch, as spirea

and peonies opened and
roses grew away
from the house, my
mother held me
on the glider

in the braid of her
arms, her green
and rose sundress
a rainbow in a breeze
of cardinals and pine,
whispered, *Honey*
and *pretty*, a
litany I couldn't
believe as I dreamed
of more, how it
wouldn't always
be like this

All the Women Poets I Like Didn't Have Their Fathers

I'm thanking you, Ben for letting me be one
too. I never could say father and still have
trouble calling anybody love. When a man touches
my skin, I just think of bed. Thank you father
for never letting me know I was pretty, for making me
need paper to say love. We never talked and last week

I met someone I wanted, I couldn't let him know.
Now I dream I write him too and the letters come back
stamped *rejected*. There's not much I trust. I know you
know what that's like—with your secret stock market
news scribbled in books like poems you couldn't show any
one, looking at trees alone too. Even with special glasses

my eyes need prisms to bend things. Still I'm sorry I never
saw what you were, what Russian pines blew behind your
eyes, or that house of chickens and goose feathers
dissolving like the print of your head from the gold
chair. No one understood why you wanted to slice
us out of your will, wanting your stocks to go on

like an eternal flame, a self investing memorial or
space ship knocked out of orbit, flashy, untouchable
as you were except here where I try to add up the pieces
as you did each meal you paid for on vacation in Cape
Cod in a small notebook you kept close to your heart
with white pills. Like that spaceship there was

a place neither of us could reach
that still circles and haunts

PHOTOGRAPH

My father sister and
I in the trees with
our hair blowing. My
sister as usual has
something in her
hands and grins in
a way no one could
say no to, dancing
in restaurants
until she pulls in
to herself at 19
like the turtles
she collects. But
here she's the sweet
pouter, my father's
pockets bulge with
things, the gum
he'll give us in
the brown chair
later reading the
funnies. I've got
a little pot and
my arms are heavy,
my father touches
us both lightly
as if he's not
sure we're real

My Sister Wants Me to Come and Read Through Thirty Years of Diaries

In the house overlooking
rain bent pines,
in the life others
would envy she loses her
self in fragments. *How
could we have changed so*
she asks over the
phone. *How could I not
still be eleven in front
of the old Plymouth
on Main Street,
Mother younger there
than I am now.* Beginnings.
What might go, pressed
flat as a daisy from
Porter Field from
someone she tries to
remember like a deaf
man remembering an
opera he heard
eleven years ago.
My sister, fragile, as
in demand as those flowers
has found her days
losing color, turning thin,
breakable as those nearly
transparent brittle leaves.
Nothing bends
like the pines. Her
days are a shelf of
blown glass buds

a heart beat could shatter. *Come*
she says *We can laugh*
at what seemed so
serious then. Maybe from
what happened in the
apartment when the
roof fell in or
at Nanny's as Herbert
was dying we can
know something about
the stories we
haven't begun yet

THE CAT'S YELP IN BLACK LIGHT

Pine needles dripping,
covering cars deeper than
mist. My sister is pulled
toward what tore night
like a child in pain
to where the cat drags
one half of his body
thrashing and tangling
through legs of chairs
no light's touched.
We wrapped his
writhing in flannel,
drove on winding roads
thru maple hills,
reaching toward noon.
Nothing to do but wait.
We were shaking, numb,
bought butter pecan
ice cream that dripped
down skin like tears.
Embolism. White pines
blackening. Next
morning the vet says
the cat died in the
night. A sack of clots,
a whole heart-full. My
sister doesn't stop
clearing the table,
packs the car, it's as
if the cat's wet fur
and twitching have
moved inside her

Holding Animals

the warm fur, like
a quilt or bunting.
Memento on the
velvet squares, a
warm potato or stones
travelers would
wrap in wool for
sleigh rides the
first night it
snowed or put in
dark beds in icy
mansions. A child
in tears burying
her neck in some
smelly dog's neck.
The waves of breath
like waves smooth-
ing ragged edges.
My aunt, after her
19 year old child
is buried clutched
the ragged black
and white cat to
her as if what she
held held her

MY UNCLE IS SELLING HIS STORE

Lazarus Department Store.
Huge stones used to sprawl
toward the tracks, a maze
of rooms over the old
bronze cash registers
and mirrors stuffed
with clothes from the
twenties. My sister and
I crouched behind walls
of shoe boxes, imagined
the leather was a fort.
Later I worked there
summers squeezing feet
into spike heels and
Keds, lacing and unlacing
what might be ahead.
I wrote pen pals, bored
with folding Ship N' Shore
blouses behind a moat of
Playtex girdle boxes,
wriggled, secretly, into
their rubber. It held
me tighter than any hands
as I dreamt of my skin
melting. Smell of damp
paint on the tin roof,
cellar of marble and
icy granite. The store
was the last place I
stopped on the way back
to Syracuse University,
snow in my hair, grabbing

stockings, lace camisole
all in peach for when I'd
be asked to do what I hadn't

My Sister Says But Doesn't *Everyone* Waste Their Life?

as Mother shrivels, as her
kingdom reaches only to the
night stand, to arranging the
way her slippers point. "So

full of the joy of life,"
someone wrote in her college
yearbook, maybe why she named
her second child Joy. Maybe

she felt it slipping from
her. My sister, blonde,
the pretty one with
boys giving her roses

and watches now sinks
back into her shell like
the turtles she cages,
covers windows to keep

out light. She reminds me
of our mother, sitting
in darkness with a
cigarette, waiting for

my call, expecting the
worst. My sister and I
chose to have cats
instead of children.

We feared becoming
what we clawed at and
bit to move away from,
as if we could help

keep genes hostage,
howling at each other
like animals caught in
traps they'd gnaw

their own legs off to escape

PHOTOGRAPHS OF MOTHERS AND DAUGHTERS

you can almost always
see the mother's hands

the daughter usually
nests in a curve of
the mother's hair or
neck like it was a cave

the way cats do the
night it starts to snow.

Some seem to suck
on the mother's breath
You might think the
mother had eyes
in her fingers

often her hands
are on the daughter's
shoulders, pulling
her close, as if

she wanted to press
her back inside

MOTHERS, DAUGHTERS

MOTHER AND DAUGHTER PHOTOGRAPHS

My mother and sister
near an old black seventies
Chevy. My sister in a
nest between my mother's
arms. You can just see
certain parts of my mother,
like a branch in a back drop.
I'm in several with
her, standing in back, her
arms around me, her prize
melon, a book just she
would write. I remember
the rabbi said enjoy
your wedding, after that
it will be your husband
and your child. I've
noticed this in several
other photos of mothers
with their girls, the
daughter held up close in
front like someone with
a desperate sign, words
pointing west or saying
Hartford. The daughter
almost blots the mother
out. It's as if there
was some huge dark hole

only a camera would pick
up where something that
had got away had been

MY MOTHER AND THE MATCHES

She said *I didn't know you
couldn't either.* My mother,
who knew which man was
circumcised and which
woman's laugh I liked

Light matches? No, we both
laugh, we couldn't. I
nearly flunked chemistry.
One day when my lab partner
didn't come, the bunsen
burner stayed unlit

At Raven's I mangle four
boxes of matches and
can't admit I'm afraid
to be burned

I spent a whole year
dreaming of fires, my
mother up April nights
sniffing for smoke. She

once said *You mean you'd
swallow it?* But she never,
until this morning, talked
about *her* fear of matches,

startling as knowing she
has a down quilt from
Odessa in a closet I've
never seen. I tell her

I never lit a candle until
lights went out for two days
in a blue cabin in Maine
and then I lit it on the wood

stove that had to be kept
burning. I hardly slept. *And
do you hate to kill flies?*
my mother asks, like Columbus
discovering a new continent

I Think of Her in a Pleated Skirt Held like a Fan

on bleachers, dark curls glitter
from under a turban or a toque, humming
"You'd be so easy to love," as the
leaves go blood thru burnt sienna in

Maryland and rumors are whispered as
lights are out in the dorm the dark
men stand at the gate of until morning.
"Yellow stars" stun. Younger than I am

now, she gets more phone calls than
the blond debutantes who say, *Hitler's right,*
but Frieda, you're different. The
blisters from her shoes flake off,

hardened skin covers her sole. Her mind is
not on Germany or politics but what
dress she'll wear for the man from Cambridge,
his pale eyes crinkle as he calls her *Angel.*

And she is humming, wishing she knew all
the words to, *so easy to love, you'd be,* as
the silver mirror darkens around the edges and
she turns a corner, holds herself where

if she wasn't braided to Baltimore, 1937
clutching the man she couldn't marry, she
might imagine me howling when she stopped, *you'd*
be so easy to, checking to see no demon with a part

in the middle of his hair and a mustache snatched me,
shrieking as I held the bars of a crib she'd
lean into nights, *to love, to love, to love …*

THAT JULY

Something under skin
crunched and sizzled as if
something else was inside.
People turned away as they
do with those who've survived
some explosion, lost their
faces and only go out at night.
My mother and I drank apricot
sours, it was all that would
stop the pain as ants bloomed
in the hot nights and I lay
flat as long as I could and
then brought the manuscripts
that had howled all summer
downstairs: diaries of the
woman who only wrote when
she left her body, women
who thought they'd been
to Mars. Lightning bugs
grazed screens and damp
walnut leaves huge as
palms that kept shaking.
Squirrels tore the pale
nuts from them as thunder
moved in and my mother
and I curled close to the
dripping lilies like
survivors who, laughing,
wash their hair in
underground streams

My Mother Who Can't

see my face clear enough
to know me in Macy's
until she hears my
voice wants to go
out in trees, look
for the comet.
She sighs that she
used to be able to
jump up from a yoga
position, now has to
catch her breath. She
wants to learn to
disco, says when
she wanted to dance
they wouldn't let her
still she danced on bare
toes as if her feet were
in pointe shoes. The
comet she says like a
child dreaming of
marzipan, we could
go out in the trees,
look up from that
brightness lashing us
with light that won't
be here again for
200 years, as she moves
by touching the
scarred red wood
slowly up stairs she
used to take three
at a time

In the Dream

My mother says look,
I'll show you why I
can't go to the party
tonight, takes off
her blouse, back
toward me. I see no-
thing, a dime sized
bump I never would
have noticed with a
cut across it. My
mother, who never
complained, cooked
venison when the
hurricane blew a
roof off a friend's
house and thirteen
people slept in our
beds the day some
thing was cut out
of her, blood still
dripping. My mother
who could open jars
no one else could,
who never stayed in
bed one day, says
the small circle
hurts. I press her
close, terrified
I'm losing what
I don't know

My Mother's Address Book

With rubber bands
flecked with powder,
slack as the face of
a child who won't
eat. Almost half
the names crossed
out with a line,
Buzzy, darkened over
with a pencil, as if there
was a rush like some
one throwing a dead
relative's shoes and
wool dresses toward
the Salvation Army
baskets, someone
catching a train,
breathlessly, the
graphite black as
shining freight

MY MOTHER STRAIGHTENING POTS AND PANS

"I can't see why you
keep so many coffee pots
with cracked handles"
she frowns as if looking
at a police line up
where all the faces
were lovers who'd
slid thru my arms
"you've go a lot of
junk but nothing
to make something hearty
you need pots that
would last a life
they don't make pots
or men as they used to"

BARNSTABLE, TWO YEARS AGO

reeds and marsh
grass, a frozen grey.
The cat locked in one
room at Murray's,
we walked, my mother
with more energy than
she'll have again
along route 1 to the
only restaurant.
Torn branches,
litter of broken
glass. We had to
yell to hear each
other over cars,
bitching, laughing
feeling sun thru
winter coats

I Looked Young a Long Time, Didn't I

My mother chortles on
the phone I shake in
front of, even before
I dial. *I never thought*
I wouldn't want to be
so skinny, she says.
In the twenties, my
mother put bands across
her 38 D breasts, was
glad I wasn't floppy
and busty. Only when
my sister was born and
she threw up for months
was she ever near 106 lbs.
Her arms always heavy
now are twigs skin
pulls away from as
if earth was sucking
on what she still hadn't
lost. I've always
held on to what's going.
Aren't you glad you
still have me? she
sings as what I thought
I couldn't go on with
out slides from me.
My mother who'd
shake her head and
sigh seeing a woman her
own age cross the
street slowly says *Honey*
I got old so fast. "You

said the same thing five
years ago and that you
felt too sick you could
never make it down last
Christmas," I joke as
if I believe in another
year I'll still be
saying this

Waxy in the moon,
almost iridescent.
My Mother and I picked
them Mother's Day in 74,

ten days after I drove
to the hospital, asked
Is my grandmother
ok? and they just said,

Go see your mother.
She said when Nanny
died, her eyes opened,
wide and totally blue,

her skin was marble.
At five, I read in a
German book of morals,
"Play with matches

and you'll burn your
mother up." I never
could strike a match
without bending it

into itself, as I
was sure I would,
crumbling without
my mother's arms.

The trillium glow in
the wind, wild, shaking.

We picked six or seven.
Next year, when they came

up I could feel the
squash of mud, see my
mother watching as I
leaped over ferns and

stones for these blood
jewels, snow flowers.
Each spring they spread
more roots. As my mother's

cheeks became caverns,
I knew the trillium
would mark more
than the spring

THE YAHRTZEIT LIGHT

Dusty, with some skeletons of
a flying thing that died
in it, as if the flame
already had been pulling
on things restless and alive.
My mother bought it, an
extra one, the year after
my grandmother died,
when my mother's hair was
still dark and curly. It
waited fifteen years, in the
middle of scales, shoe
polish and liquids to make
what is glowing hot, spit
eerie light and the flicker
of death into shadows. I
couldn't throw it out:
more Jewish than anything
I owned and wondered if my
mother would have other
people leaving too fast to
say goodbye to, rub her
hands in front of this
candle, rub what was still
warm numb as a heart rubbed
raw. This morning, my mother
at ninety pounds, was afraid to
stay alone in the mall,
her face grey as the stone
squares she had trouble,
even holding my arm, getting
across. I take her bag, as

if alone she might collapse
and nobody would know who
she was to claim her. My
uncle's voice on tape
reminds it's the anniversary
of my mother's mother's death
so tonight I give the candle
to her, go down to the room
where no candle could catch.
In the glitz of fire, my
mother's cheeks are caverns
no light fills

STAYING IN MY MOTHER'S APARTMENT THE FIRST TIME WITHOUT HER

The last postcard I
mailed to her on the
refrigerator next to
phone numbers where
I might be. Dusters
and dust. I should
have known something
was wrong when she
said she was *too lazy*
to go to the Post
Office, too tired to
get the emerald green
sweater and skirt I
sent when she wrote
she was starved for
something green. She
wore it once, New
Year's Eve she could
not swallow. My books
behind glass, my
letters in a drawer
with wintergreen life
savers she only
recently lost her
taste for under photo
graphs with her legs
so plump ten of her
shrivelled thighs
could fit inside one,
her black eyes
laughing and the

clock that staggers
forward a few minutes,
then falls backward

Nichols Lodge in the Rain. Or, the Night before My Mother and I Will Take the Ambulance Back to My House, the Last Night I Will Spend without Her until the Fall

Corn tassels bending,
holly hocks, gladiolus
lopped. It's as if the
lettuce had fallen
down for rose zinnias
to kneel on, heads
lowered under the grey.
The Rose of Sharon
dripping, tiger lilies,
beans at the altar of
rain the white spike
flowers hallelujah
up from. Sun flowers
lean against wet wood

On the night before
what I know will be my
mother's last visit, I
try to soak up gladiolus,
violets, all that grows
as my mother just grows
thinner. Jade chrysanthemum
stalks blur shasta daisies,
roses, glistening plums.
Black locusts drip. Rain
flattens sweet peas as
blood grows into the maples
three hours south of
where my mother waits

Green vines, a bracelet
around the wet barnwood
as white bells on the
sills poke up from leaves
that could be shamrocks
or clover. I could use
a 4th leaf spurting in
the grey before what
will be over in a
script I can only
wildly imagine
starts to start

MY MOTHER WANTS LAMBCHOPS, STEAKS, LOBSTER, ROAST BEEF

something to get
her teeth in
forget the shakes
cancer patients
are supposed to
choose, forget
tapioca pudding
vanilla ice
she wants what
is full of blood
something to
chew to get
the red color
out of something
she can attack
fiercely. My
mother who never
was namby pamby
never held her
tongue never
didn't attack
or answer back,
worry about
angering or hurt-
ing anybody but
said what she
felt and wouldn't
walk any tight
rope, refuses the
pale and delicate
for what's blood

what she can
chew even spit
out if she
needs
to

MY MOTHER AND THE LILACS

Their purple meant
spring. "That whole
apartment was
lilacs," she glows,
retelling how
the one she
couldn't marry
but checks for
in phone books
fifty years
surprised her
with orchid
and snow. She
wishes for a yard,
for daughters
who will plant
lilacs that
bloom, not just
stunted twigs
shadowed by pine.
Unlike card games,
where the one
with nothing wins,
what never bloomed
haunts the most

CURLING ON THE BOTTOM OF MY MOTHER'S BED

as she would
on mine in
different houses,
bring me iced tea
at midnight or
cold chicken we'd
devour with our
fingers after
a date. I don't
think she minded
having to take
my arm in dark
restaurants
or crossing the
street, a good
reason to touch
me as she does
more freely now
as light in June
starts shrivelling.
We whisper to
each other these
past 41 days we
haven't been apart,
like new lovers
who feel what
they have so rare
they can't bear
to sleep apart

My Mother Listens to Classical Music

As she didn't
always, preferring
talk radio. Schubert,
and Bizet, Chopin
as if words were
too charged, now
too hard to hold
on to. Minor notes
in Bloch soothe,
a hand on a burning
forehead. I like
the wash of adagios,
what's moving slow,
stretching, not
jarring as so
much is lately. You
can take this
radio my mother
says, it gets tv.
I don't want it I
say lying here
with notebook and
paper and she says
"not now, after
I'm gone."

GETTING MY MOTHER ICE

Nothing lasts long
in this heat
except the dark
of waiting. At
2 am or 3 or
4 I lead her
like a child
with a night
mare to the
bathroom across
the hall. If I
don't get the
wash cloth
right, not too
wet, or hot
or soapy, she
will refuse
demerol, lie
moaning, "I
can't." It
seems those
words are
my words

TAKING MY MOTHER TO THE BATHROOM

I lead her, a
child waking up
from a nightmare.
dazed by light.
She lags, hurries
then, half cranky,
half grateful.
She wants the
door shut, then
says open it,
wants my hands
the right way,
wash in between
my fingers. She
says the wash
cloth is too
wet, too cold,
too soapy. The
towels are too
heavy. You don't
she spits, cover
your mouth. Go
home, you should
not be here to
see me like this

MY MOTHER'S TWEEZERS

Like her silver
curls, the hairs
she didn't want
grew thicker too.
Maybe something
in the i.v. jump
started shoots
of hair that
months before
a hairdresser
sliced off in a
style my mother
hated, said, "was
killing her." I
cringed thinking,
"Mama, it will
still grow when
you can't."
Her main wish
besides a trip
to New York City
was for a warm
bath in her own
house. She longed
to polish
the porcelain
tub that held
her better than
most arms, that
pale shrine she
knelt to clean
as if it was an

altar. And then
to curl in a thick
towel with the
tweezers she
said she couldn't
bear losing, as if
she could pluck all
the dark in her out

Am I Talking to Hair or to a Person:

"Brush your hair away,"
my mother demanded,
"I want to see you."

I think how an uncle,
dead since the fifties,
would beg me to wear it up
before he died, yanked
into a bun as English Department
professors sneered it should be

One dead poet wrote
I was his hair house.

I heard that after years
of nagging about lipstick and hair,
after you have come to expect it
(even choose what you know
will bring these attacks on),

the parent, old maybe,
or weak or sick, lets go.
The strength to notice,
a luxury of health.

My mother on i.v. and
unable to eat for four days,
dozes off after demerol,
then jolts up to ask if she's
talking to hair or to a person

And this time I'm glad
she still wants to change me.

MINT LEAVES AT YADDO

In frosty glasses of
tea. Here, iced
tea is what we
make waiting for

death with this
machine my mother
wanted. Not knowing
if she'd still be

here for her birth-
day we still shopped
madly, bought her
this iced tea maker for.

For twenty days my
mother shows only
luke warm interest
in presents or tea,

vomits even water,
but I unpack the
plastic, intent
on trying this

sleek device while
my mother, queen
of gadgets—
even a gun to

demolish flies—
maybe the strangest

thing she got me,
can still see the

tall glasses that
seem summery on what
is the longest day.
Soon the light

will go she says
the days get shorter.
I can't bear, she
murmurs, another

winter in Stowe and
I think how different
this isolation is,
this iced tea, this

time that stretches
where little grows
as it did, green
as that mint, except

my mother, smaller
more distant, gaunt

My Mother's Ring

Once too tight
now it swivels on
her bony finger.
Only her knuckles
bulge. I can't
do it, my mother
says, a shriveled
bird in the stark
hospital bed. When
I saw the dead bird
in Morristown I
felt it was a sign.
In two weeks my
mother's mouth
is so dry it curls
as if full of wild
feathers. The ring
glitters, spits
out a yellow light,
not anywhere near
as pure as the
myth of its per-
fection my mother
spun of it like
whatever else
pleased her,
like me

PUTTING MY MOTHER TO BED

She's shaking, shivering
when I pull the green
sweat shirt over her
head, wants a panty

liner, just in case.
She laughs, says she can
remember the first time she
used the new kind, tried

to stick Care Free to her,
not her underwear. The mood
changes when I give her
the pill she doesn't

want, says it stuck, makes
her worse. She's sure she
is choking. I rub her back
feel her bones jut out

skeletal nearly, rub the
back of her neck under
her hair, hoping she won't
spit the pill out. Leaving

her bed I walk past the dark
room we hung helium balloons
in, for her birthday, as much
for ourselves as for her

as if to see something light
and floating. Bears and

clowns that could, if one
let go of them, like

birds you pay a few cents for
in India, not to amuse or
feed you, but to be
set free, like

someone holding on because
they feel you pulling on
them, holding
them, float up

brush their color against
you as they escape

WHEN I PUT ON HER FUR COAT

I'm wrapping in
another's skin,
feeling that
body is a cloth
the cold will
enter so nothing
more will dis-
solve. I put her
around me, her
kleenex in
pockets, her
wintergreen
mints. The
past becomes
thinner, more
transparent. I
see thru it
back to when I
wouldn't have
put something
like this
on. *Mama*
I yelp to wake
myself up, bring
the coat to
bed, spreading
it like it was
hair over the
quilt where
we peeled
oranges, the
smallest slices

the babies she
smiled. Then I
settle under the
dark as she is

AFTERWARD, GOING TO MY MOTHER'S APARTMENT

posters from my
readings in the
hallway, the
living room. My
photographs in the
only glassed in
case, the only
shelves not dusty
or covered with
powder as if it
snowed through
July, didn't just
freeze over. This
museum I always
knew would with
its care-taker
gone haunt even
more: coupons,
years of canceled
checks, a partial.
I put her night
gown on, don't
change the sheets
or even move her
kleenex off the
bed, just to one
side then open
the jewel music
box. Only two
notes play and
then it's quiet

OBITUARY

Others' parents
die. My father
falls on his
face in the snow,
stains December.
But my mother's
obit is a shot
gun, machete.
Aids virus in
needles I clutch,
a tree crashing
thru the roof,
pulling wires
that sizzle and
light up night
like KKK flames
loud as Crystal
Night or The
Challenger, I'm
the car that
she's in that
plunges into
rock and steel
as the bridge
we're on lets go

THE DAUGHTER I DON'T HAVE (1)

could be my other.
I see her face in
the shape of mine
in each metro
car flashing by, her
brown eyes drink
me in. I could be
walking into my
reflection in the
mirror, see her
cock her head as
I do, squint to
read in dim light
where she hides in
the jacket of a
book with my name
on it, in the spoon
my mother brought
me from Chicago
World's Fair. She's
with me in the ferns,
a siamese twin I
can't quite touch.
She knows my heart
beat, shares secrets
in my blood, is
the figure in a
paper weight the
snow won't settle in

THE DAUGHTER I DON'T HAVE (2)

jolts up in the
middle of the night
to curl closer than
skin, pink tongued
in a flannel dress
I wore once in some
story. I part her
hair, braid her
to me as if to
keep what I can't
close, like hair
wreathes under
glass in New
England. Or maybe
pull the hair into
a twist above the
nape of her neck,
kiss what's exposed
so wildly part of
her stays with me

THE DAUGHTER I DON'T HAVE (3)

wouldn't dwell on
nightmares, on
her parents only
touching under
stone. She wouldn't
cringe years before
that at her mother's
birth date on granite
with a dash to be filled
in. My girl wouldn't
vow to never have what
she could lose, hoard
loss like diamonds
in a safe deposit box,
expensive but useless.
She wouldn't wake
up before the first
rose light, remember
death dates but forget
an uncle's birthday.
The digital clock
wouldn't burn 9:37 into
her like a tattoo as
someone she loved
stopped breathing.
She'd see what was
ahead like a yard of
new snow her steps
would make designs in

THE DAUGHTER I DON'T HAVE (4)

won't rip her father
out of the photograph
where their hands are
so intertwined each
loses something of
himself. She won't
tear one half into
confetti or think
how night streets
filled with bits
of paper at the
end of the war,
wish her father
had been away so
maybe he could
come back home to
her. My daughter
wouldn't walk
around the apart-
ment for the last
time years later,
touch where his
head touched the
yellow chair and
left its shape
nights he said
nothing, mute as
a nightingale that
never's heard an-
other nightingale
sing, wouldn't
imagine his face,

hands on her
shoulders behind
her so vividly
she hangs cloth
over the mirror
as if in a house
for the dead. Each
poem she writes,
a kaddish for him

THE DAUGHTER I DON'T HAVE (5)

could counterfeit my
face and sighs. She
puts on my cashmere
from college, my
new sheer baby T.
She's clever, out
wits me as only a
good counterfeiter
can. She used to
leave her hair in
the sink. Now she's
more subtle but she
still plays tricks,
hooks a belt on the
hole I'd never use
so I won't forget
her. Her profit
comes from watching
me squirm, knowing
if I'd just made a
reproduction of my
self, she wouldn't
have to spy on me,
tend to details,
perfecting what is
not real so well
she never may be
recognized

THE DAUGHTER I DON'T HAVE (6)

hovers over the lilacs,
a cloak over plum
branches then moves
like a warm front
east. She is that
buzz in the night
out of reach in
blackness. I've known
her sting, how she
tangles in my hair,
that with me, she
will forget I fought
her, forget her
wandering and
waiting like bees
that lose all memory
of their old hive
once they've swarmed

THE DAUGHTER I DON'T HAVE (7)

is the one my mother
said, without, I
won't know what heart
ache is. She trails
me on buses. My
mother's given her
the key to who I am
and she's enough
frequent flyer miles
to follow me my
whole life. She could
find a better mother,
one with more room
in her life but she's
as stubborn as I am.
Branches scraping
the roof are her
fingers begging me
to let her in,
the rain's her crying.
She calls me cruel,
dials my phone then
hangs up before
it's light. She
thinks I'll give in
though I insist that
it is just my love
that keeps me from
making her mine

OTHER PEOPLE

BLISSFUL MISFITS AND SECRET FACES
(OTHER PEOPLE)

JEANNE MARIE PLOUFFE

(after reading Carolyn Forché)

Small and dark behind your mother's full skirts
as she cleaned other people's houses.
Florence and I imagined worms slithered thru you
when you ate lumps of sugar in my grandmother's
bathroom, still stayed thin. Eyes like cloves

under huge lashes in classes you wouldn't say
a word in. *Canuck* the boys called out
over Otter Creek Bridge as your legs got less
spindly and the girls from college professors'
homes didn't invite you. People said your last name

with the tone they'd say tramp. Your skin creamy,
your hair curled with night. There wasn't a boy
who didn't think he could put his hand inside
your dress. You never said anything,
as if a part of you was already gone,

as if there was some place to go. Once,
singing of Quebec, your eyes gleamed like the gold
cross boys yanked from your neck and tossed in the snow.
I hear the trailer burned down, the survivors
headed north. Jeanne Marie, if you read this

please write me

167

THE LANAE, HOTEL KAIAMONA

The Japanese girl
waiting 7 hours
under the hau tree
holds the same
drink, watches thru
its water. The sand
blackens. Diamond
Head eats the sun. She
twists hair like a
ring around her
finger. Pink
leaves brown
on the floor. She
is telling of those
apples in the mountain
that don't need cold
like plums but sweeter,
smiles but she
won't leave, come
with us, stays tho
the candles are burning,
is like those birds
in Africa that fly
for hours hardly beating
their wings but they
can't land, crash
breaking their
beaks, blinded maybe
and paralyzed
going around in
shock back and
forth to their nests
not understanding

GEORGIA O'KEEFFE

I painted my first skull

from a barrel of bones

the cow's head
against the blue

I like the shapes
they have no
thing to do with death

mountains thru the
holes in a bone

bones against the sky
bones and moons
bones and flowers
a reddish bone with a yellow sky

The Knife Thrower's Woman

I think of other things.
Once I itched so in the
middle of a throw but
I thought of words from
something in an old hymn.
I know the shape his
fingers take when
the steel slips thru
them, think of them
outside my clothes and
then unbuttoning and
stroking and sliding. We
never talk about
being afraid. His
sweat isn't from
any heat. I step away
from the knife handles
like a snake shedding
its skin. It's not
me he sees. I am
the space, his snow
angel shadow in the snow
where something has been

He Said He Was in the Men's Room at the Airport, a William Buckley Story

it might come as a
surprise to some but
William actually has
to use them sometimes.
Well, I was there. It
wasn't, if you know
what I mean, a time
to say *Hi Bill*. He
might think I was
putting the moves
on him. He was there
first so when he
leaves I'm doing
still what I've done
50 years, don't need
to keep my eyes
down there so I
look up, off to the
right, naturally I
see him walking away,
about to leave. He
goes to the sink but
he doesn't wash his
hands. Look I'm still
standing there about
to zip but I don't
need to jerk my head
back, it's nothing new
I'm doing. Buckley's
shutting off the tap.
The hot then the cold

and he goes to the
next sink, looks and
does the same thing.
He goes to each of
the seven sinks but
never washes his hands,
just makes sure not a
faucet is dripping.
I guess even when
it comes to water,
maybe even soap
he's a conservative

ELAINE

in the photographs
you're tan and slim
only the latest
tiny bikini to show
your perfect pared
down curves. For
days you'd eat ice
to squeeze into
the you you wanted.
I was afraid to
slither thru the
room, your tongue
a whip. My cheeks
stung where you
slapped with a
scowl that summer
at Champlain where
I longed for your
straight black hair.
Even your mother
toed the line when
you ranted in the
middle of supper,
would leap up to iron
some little white
piqué shorts you
might need. Your
sister never had
such white teeth. I
hated you but dreamed
of being as thin.
You even bossed

the flowers. As
queen of 4 sons you
must have reigned,
married of course
to a doctor. When I
heard they'd sliced
the second sweet
breast away that
pressed like a nose
up in the air in
to pale cotton,
I couldn't believe
anything of yours
could have grown
that far from
your control

Nuns at a Retreat

they'd hoist up their black
skirts she said years
later when she left, it
was like a group of children
or strange birds all
ruffling black feathers
letting their black stockinged
legs dry off as they kicked
on the stones
looking at each other's
thighs and calves. It was
as if the sun was making
love to them

HE SAID HE SAW MY PICTURE IN ROLLING STONE

When he called, said he
wanted to explain the
situation, that he was
a cross between Jagger
and a thin Max Von Sydow

he said he had to tell me
he was a famous, a rock
star until it bored him
wanted me to send him
photographs, forget

the poems, 3 or 4 perfect
nudes and said if he liked
them as much as my face—
asked first, did I have
flabby skin a 90 year old

body, ass like the girl he got
from some porno mag. He
wanted to make sure I'd
never had a baby, my age
then he'd send me an

airline ticket and
maybe we could. It was my
face he said got to him. Jane
Fonda's skin's too
oily he said he didn't

like bodies that drooped
or brown eyes since his

mother gave him away.
He knew he could do
anything, beat up
some famous poet

Poetry is too easy
he said he was light
but dark on the
inside, asked me to read
a sexy poem and would
I mind if he came
on the phone imagining
my he was sorry it wasn't

a taller body. The woman
from the porno rag had
paid her own money to
meet him, took off

her clothes in a bar
but she wouldn't do.
Not much got to him.
But my face looked
like one that would

Was I a model he
asked, did I know I
looked like Dylan's
ex wife? Had I
done it with women

in an airline wash
room, with four in bed?
Was I raped ever, did
I have a hooked nose?
Was I Jewish? He wanted

to be sure truck
drivers turned when I
crossed the street.
He went on. Finally
I guess his hand got
sticky. I should have
but I couldn't
hang up

THE EROTIC MIRROR

(from the Governor's Motor Inn)

Under glass in the museum
like women's clothes
from Plains Cree
hung behind glass,
still stained with bloody
holes from arrows.
In boudoirs, bordellos
and honeymoon hotels
people have used mirrors
for erotic pleasure,
the visual stimulation
of looking at one's self
and one's partners as
objects of desire. But
I think of the young
girl lured here by a
man twice her age
who she saw do sports
on tv in high school
and walked out of the
room never imagining
a heart shaped
bed she'd see her
breasts and thighs
split on in the
mirror above as
she skidded like
a skater feeling her
blade slip one
second into the
Olympic final

over red velvet
pillows in terror.
Only when his snores
make ripples in the
water under them
and she can watch light
glitter in the prisms'
ice, see her thighs
are not ugly, that her
hair is cut maple
sun slides over on
the sheets does she
find anything pleasing

THE WOMAN WHO CANNED HANDS, SOMETIMES FINGERS

As if to always
have a supply,
have them on
hand. Fingers
to calm, hold
her. She could
have pickled a
husband's fists
as a reminder, a
warning or put
up lovers' fingers
in salt and dill
to open when snow
banked the door.
Her father never
touched her. Her
mother held on
so tight there
are claw marks.
Then there were
light fingered
men who worked
fast in gloves,
left no trace.
Sometimes she put
skin peeled from
a hand in jars
like souvenirs
of snakes who
left what they
were behind them

or perfume bottles
only an amber
stain lingers
in from what
was sweet

She Waits like Some Sharp Cheddar in the Pantry

huddling in the dark
on the shelf
less exotic
maybe than
women flashy as
Camembert,
intense as St Andre's
soft cheese,
less outgoing
and sure of their
direction than
women who know
who they are,
like Jarlsborg or
Swiss, clean cut,
in suits, sipping
chardonnay as
leaves go blood
and burnt sienna.
She prides
herself on being
free of holes a
tongue or finger
could get stuck
in. Only her
thighs soften,
so long alone,
still creamy as
Havarti, as blue
spreads under wraps
where what ripens
is dying

OLD MEN HOTEL BRENNER

they are like plants
put out on the porch
that only bloom at

night when the light
won't burn those
leaves that dissolve

by morning. Chairs
and teeth click.
Smells of garlic,
roses the word

"yesterday" like a
pile of bones a
necklace of stories
they thread with
their own hair
from these strings
they make a

harp to play
in the snow as
the holidays
blur. Those who

don't come back
next August are
added, become
strings for the
fingers left
to touch

THE OLD WOMAN IN AMSTERDAM

like someone who feels
she'll be pressed in
the dark of earth
who walks with all
her windows open,
nude, skin flapping
like fingers signing
in a house of blind
men. She cuts maples
to stubs to let sun
eat her, leaves
shutters open in rain
to feel her hair flow
like linden dust,
doesn't want anything
heavy as earth on her
yet. She sleeps on
top of a pile of blue
quilts as if her life
was leaves resting on a
lake fish drift up
in thru dark water

THE PRESIDENT'S THIGHS HIDE OUT IN THE ROSE GARDEN

before rhinestones
evaporate from
jade petals,
they hide their

white under navy,
pale as a chrysalis,
then coil under
linen trying to

lose their accent,
their flab. One
rubs the other
as if clapping.

Dark cloth like
a bundling board
in some snow covered
New England farm house

circa 1792 where
two slept under
the same quilt
but with pine

between them
still wanting what
they wanted but
pressed to stay pure

The President's Arms Are like Oak Branches

spread out further
than you'd imagine
they could reach
without splintering

they propel whoever
is within them
into his chest hair
or toward each

other's chins and
hips so it seems
he's all a curve
of flesh. When

they hang by his
side, they are enormous,
tall as a child
he could hoist above

him as if tossing
feathers before
they fold into navy
wool without a life

like an octopus
out of its element,
its tentacles dangling
by its side,

uneasy with nothing
to wrap around

THE BLIND BASKET MAKER

pulling reeds
into what can
hold peat and

linen in a
cottage with
stone floors

the sea from
his window, he
hasn't seen it

since he was 5
weaves willows
into baskets

knows the color
by the thickness
of the reeds

he says in the
wind they have
separate voices

that they sound
as different as
different women

The Man Who Is Married to Siamese Twins Joined at the Skull

In our huge bed
from a bird's eye view
we look like a three
petaled flower.
I rub my wife's
neck. It's always
sore from leaning
over in chairs, on
trains, walking thru
the aisles of the
A & P. We're happy,
the three of us. Her
sister shuts us out
when I get to
rutting loud in her.
Then we all sing
oh where oh where
has my little
dog gone in the
shower and I
bring them both
hot chocolate.
We can lie on our
backs with the
tv swinging
from the ceiling
and laugh at the
news. Her sister
threatens to
run off and I kiss
her soundly. They

think the same
jokes are funny.
Sometimes when my
wife is asleep I talk
to her sister. She
can't imagine
what it would be
like to be separated,
have half of her
sliced away

Alberta Hunter

you could hear
Bessie Smith
from here to
49th St

I've got the first
record I made
on Black Swan, ran

away from home
away from Beale St
working at a night
club called Dream
land brother Louis
Armstrong, up to
play 2nd trumpet
his first wife
collapsed died
at her husband's
funeral, I love

church but until
they put that sand
and dirt in my face
ladies and gentle
men I've had enough

MURIEL RUKEYSER ACCEPTING AN HONORARY DEGREE

with the night smelling of
rain that hasn't started.
Damp leaves, a mist where
there will be roses. Muriel,
with her hair slicked black
like someone trying never
to hide anything, a figure
head on a ship, hair blown
away from the sea wind.
The room is a hot rustle
of programs. Black robes,
black skirts and white
blouses. Bright red silk
rings beneath her robe
like a smile or a wave.
Her face uplifted near
the podium is that of
a woman looking up at a
lover, opening, feeling
sun warm on her skin
and the air all lilacs,
who feels July stretch
ahead like route 107
in Kansas, knows this
minute is everything

THE UGLIEST WOMAN TO THE PAINTER WHO TURNED HER DOWN ON THE STREET

when she asked
for ten dollars then
5, then 2.50.
For God's sake
just take me
and he did,
to his mother,
begged her to
get this woman
a job, said
"Girl, you're
in the wrong
occupation."
"I know what
I look like,"
she said. "If
you can see beauty
in what others
can't, you'll
be ok. But, if
not, forget
painting, *you're*
the one in the
wrong occupation."

sees herself in
the mirror, a
dummy, there
for others to
pounce on, shove
their mouth into
her mouth. Some
where else, she
remembers when
she was in white
lace, wore her
name like a jewel,
a sapphire, or
garnet. Now she
feels used, spread
out for strangers,
then, packed
away. Her face
shows where she's
been, marred
as old shoes.
It's like a gang
bang, this CPR
party, strange
men bouncing on
her as if she
didn't have a
heart, pinching
her nostrils,
shoving their
breath inside
as if they
were gods

HE'D RATHER HAVE A PAPER DOLL

a porn woman. I'd
soak in a tub of bath
oil an hour, come back
and drop the towel and
he'd roll over. Even
on our honeymoon, he
was out getting skin
flicks. He had *Playboy*
and *Penthouse*. Then,
things in brown envelopes
stashed behind furniture,
films, I was in competition
even that week in Los
Vegas but I tried
eight and a half years.
I had my breasts done,
belly, but he'd lock him
self in the bathroom for
3 hours. I could hear
paper turning. He said it
had nothing to do with
me. And he'd been such a
gentleman. Five dates
before he even kissed me.
My father told his three
girls men just want one
thing. I wear teddies to
bed, eyelashes. I tried
suicide twice, never told
anyone, thought if I just
bought the right nylon
or lace. A real woman

scares him. On paper, he
can have as many, never
with cellulite, or scars
or hair where it should
not be, doing what
ever he can imagine

SOUTH OF HERE

No leaves turn rust
or apricot. Air's
a fog of dogwood
and peach. Kudzu
takes a breath and
keeps on. No chill
is deep enough to
make words clot,
make bells thick
as ragged branches
slashing air. A
waitress, Donna
Muriella, slips
vanilla rose long
finger nails thru
frost tipped hair,
smiles too fast.
The light falls
away like blood
sun in choke
cherries. We've
driven numbly,
even our faces
in spoons seem
someone else's.
Wednesday blurs,
spills into green.
We move on thru
Blue Ridge and
Climax, half
feel the suck
of water in thick

wet wind. Clouds,
moan of leaves
on stone like
the slurred
accent of that
bleached out
waitress

Under the Rose

lips remind us of those
lips down there you
said once, kissing the
back of an envelope with
red gloss. Your mirror
had a wreathe of men
drawn by the suck of
your soft whispers, a
tongue they read the
braille of. Cold comfort
you wrote me more
years later than we
were then. Still, I
envied how their
mouths looked for
any mouth of yours,
the silk and slippery
so many thought came
from your heart. You
had parasols from
exotic night clubs I
was insulted I looked
too young to be served
in. Lara, your room
always smelled of
scent, while mine
reeked of paint and
glue for some science
project. You took
so many sailors'
pea coats in your
hand, pulled them to

you. Now I hear you
had enough, as if you
outlived your own
curiosity and what I
longed for put you
to sleep. None of
those lovers could
fill you. At the end,
you left even your
children as if every
thing stuffed into you
gnawed until what
glittered was like a
mine so scooped of
rubies it collapsed

PICASSO STANDING NEAR SOME GERMANS AFTER HE PAINTED GUERNICA

one of the
officers
asked him

"is it you
who did that?"

"No," Picasso said,
"it was

you"

The Jesuit Who Doesn't Care for Money

places orders to
long haired poets
for books, charges
them to the library.
He begs for strands
of long hair for
a bookmark, to
wrap around his
finger so his
finger will smell
where it's been,
writes for used
underwear, a life
saver that's ridden
all night inside
those lips down
there he calls
on the invoice
his devotional
objects

THE JESUIT WHO WRITES AROUND

is bold in his
small cell like
someone making
obscene phone
calls from a
closet. He
writes in Italian
for strands of hair
from 77 women. First
he mentions the
weather, says he
never had genital
sex but is an
expert on back
rubs. He sends his
photo with the
Pope says he's
praying for you,
sends 20$ for
something of yours
he can hold like
a cross for
ecstasy

She Said She Could See Music

didn't everyone?
shapes in blue or
golds she felt
them wrapping her
it was moving into
a garden only
the smells were
colors it
wouldn't be as
rich if it
was only sounds
it would be
flat she'd
be lonely with
out the swirls the
rose and tourmaline
the emerald
not confusing
not at all
not anymore
than seeing and
hearing might
seem to
someone blind

Falling to the Ground, He Traces Stars

light is
bending into the hills.
This day unwinding. How dark moves in now.
Close by and uncertain,
he watches shadow and light
print your body,
how your flesh is shining, moon-pale.
Fresh herbs and seeds and the bright leaves folding,
briars grey in the distance.
Stillness. Birdless. The quiet river.
And your head on his thigh
is lovely, startling. As if to keep him
from sleep, the curve of your back
draws him in. And your warm
hair that smells of flowers pulls him
tight against your skin.
Later, you twist
away, coil from this last sun. Nothing stays
but earth chill. Grass in his hand
disarms him. Restless
and falling to the ground beside you, he traces how far away
    the stars have grown,
and those dark mouths that live in your sleep.
O Eve, do you dream how your terrible sighs blind him

BARGAIN

She all the time rationalizing
nagging about how if
they couldn't afford to
it was one thing
but not being tied
down, no children yet
nor family to think of
and rent being free
and their food too,
others had,
it really couldn't be
much to pay for
bliss and all
that went along with it.
He, knowing her
womanly calculations
plainly wrong, but
her eyes pleading so
and the day very hot,
went along with her and
ate the bitter apple

FLAMING BRACELETS
(BARBIE, MAD GIRLS, LORENA AND JESUS)

THE MAD GIRL DIALS VICTORIA'S SECRET AFTER MIDNIGHT

She never did this before
she whispers to herself
as she used to to men
who wondered why she called
a Dial a Date show
on radio, drove thru
the unlit street in town
to drink vodka with a
bummed out Viet Nam
vet. Something churns
in her, won't let her
sleep. She wants some
thing to wrap around, to
curve into her curves,
longs to treat herself,
relax, slip into some
warm safe place as she
finds it gets harder
to do with anyone
around. She imagines her
self sprawled on satin
like the centerfold
models waiting not for
a tongue or hands but
for lace, silk, the
softest cotton in

periwinkle and blush
to bring her color,
as she moves,
a second skin
like a lover who's
a superb fit

THE MAD GIRL PICKS INACCESSIBLE MEN

deaf men she tries
to sing to or those with
bodies burned so they couldn't
tell her fingers were near,
if the lights weren't blaring.
She picks men in love with
Sigourny Weaver who moan
too often at huge breasts
as she curls into her 102
pounds. Now only she
warms the place filled
by her body. If she could
lay the men out sideways
it would be farther than
she could walk in a
week, especially this
October when leaves pull
off like someone who held
her leaving town. And
though she thinks their
gold will camouflage the
grey like the false
light covering the window,
where they touched is like
where those branches scrape stones
off the roof, leave
holes. She buys an orchid
angora sweater for the
man she'll just see in
court instead of bread,
sprays lilac on a letter to
the Supreme Court. Night slips

into the holes and hardens,
stirs up the tapeworm inside
her no arms or fingers
can feed

The Mad Girl Remembers White Umbrellas, River Boat Jazz

as ice clinked in a
sweating glass
and banjos and strings
pressed fingers
like nipples.
The war went
on and off in other
countries, the boats
burned. The baby
swells under the
fringed chemise,
would play with the
feather boa, watch
lily pads in the
churn of steam
as Spanish moss
dripped into almond
and cantaloupe water
and the moon in
her diamond was as
much a mirage
as all this

THE MAD GIRL NEEDS MORE THAN MOST OTHERS

more sleep to dream
of those blue mists
off fjords past Oslo
where tracks she made
in December fill
more paper to type
out the blue of
afternoons in still
rooms. The fringe of
a teal carpet is all
that changes from
Wednesday to Wednesday.
She needs more quilts
to sweat under, more
blankets of rust and
aquamarine, more calls,
more lips to rub the
crease smooth under her
eyes, more leather
boots in grey and
fawn, licorice and
ivory to run from
herself in

The Mad Girl Feels She's on a Leash, Could Be in a Hotel in Leningrad

a lover's blue car
circles like cheap blue and
gold plastic bracelets 3 for
four dollars in Woolworth's
or cameras in the wall
while her mother phones
on the hour pleading for
train schedules, the exact
hours she might wash her
hands. Even the quilt's
bugged she's sure as she
plots to leap past booby
traps and bugs into sheets that
would soothe, not just hold
her too tight. *I've left
town two days early* she
telegraphs the night, bites
the phone wire into 14 white
worms, lets stillness
flood Thursday like the
body of a young tanned
boy just beginning to
taste lust washed up
on a Florida beach after
a freeze turns oranges soft

Barbie Watches TV Alone, Naked

She's got her
bride clothes
on the floor, her
cancan skirt,
pale ruffly fish
net tights and a
cameo choker
tossed around the
bed like a moat.
Now she's got
the remote control
clicker and can
switch and change,
not be at someone
else's whim, her
body twisted,
dressed and un-
dressed, a slave
to another's
fingers as if her
ankles were bound
in leather, chained,
legs spread apart.
Travel Around the
World with Barbie
stamped on her fore-
head in catalogues
from Sears. She is
sick of having
a rod jammed up in
side her, of being
boxed in with a

hair brush that
usually goes where
it shouldn't. She
wants to lie in
tv light, not have
to hide what she is
missing: a belly
button, skin that
smells like skin,
doesn't want to
have to keep smiling
as any stranger who
buys her twists her
arm out of its socket
or throws her out

Barbie Hunts thru Medical Books Looking for What Is Wrong with Her when She Sees Her Birth Date in a Book, Knows She Is Over 30

and feels so
hollow inside,
unfulfilled,
as if all she's
done is change
her clothes.
She wonders a
bout the women's
movement, maybe
she frowns it's
the change and
she hasn't even
had a baby, had a
period, a
hair that was
not in place.
Perfection that
can be shelved,
one yank and I'd
be bald, naked.
She flips thru
chapters on
neurosis, wonders
if it's hormones
she lacks. Where
she's been, hardly
seems to matter:
the beach, Sun
Valley, Spain.
It's all facade,

going thru the
motions. What
did a wedding
get me she groans
I never was free
moving, as they
said in 1975
but empty, full
of holes—some
thing just for
someone else
to collect
or abuse

BARBIE WONDERS ABOUT BUYING A COFFIN

if she'll need one,
not that these
plastic boxes she's
in so long on a
shelf aren't like
being buried in a
toy box under eaves,
freezing in winter,
scorched by June.
She wonders if they
will bury her in a
ballerina costume,
a rodeo suit, if
they'll shave her
hair or braid it.
Just because she's
empty doesn't mean
she doesn't care. Or
that her velvet or
tulle, even her under
pants have been stripped
from her and she was
left nude as some
one in the camps
about to march into
gas, doesn't mean
she doesn't want
to know if she'll
go with one of her
many scarves around
her, à la Isadora.
or if Ken, supposing

she's eyeing a Ricky
or P.T. or Alan,
even trying Christy,
rages in, beans her
with his boogie board,
strangles her with
the ropes of his
Hawaiian fun hammock
or poisons her with
cyanide in soda
from the All American
store, runs her over
in a remote control
Corvette and leaves
her in the trunk
with nothing to wear
for this last stop

NAVY BARBIE

wants to see the world,
she does get a little
seasick but likes
the white uniform, tho
the skirt is a little
too loose and long for
her taste. Still it might
be a change she can go
with. Actually, the sequins
dug into her shoulders,
the ballerina tulle
scratched, and tho it was
kept secret, fun fur
made her sneeze. And
forget the Parisian
Bonjour look: that was
the worst, a cameo
choker size of a plum
or a small coconut
wedged against her larynx,
so she says when I tried
to say yes or no it
scraped, and the lace
under my arms—talk
about sandpaper. But
the worst was those fish
net hose, rough, and the
garter, Jesus, grating,
my toes burned from that
pattern, crammed into
high-heeled platform
open-toes and the hair

piece with feathers. At
least in the Navy they've
actually, she smiles,
given me something to
read. My hair is natural.
I'm authentic. First
Class Petty Officer.
I finally am more than
just a pretty: I rank

LORENA HEARS HER PENIS CALLING FOR HER

moaning like a baby
left in the reeds,
vulnerable as a little
Moses, bobbing along
in a basket on his own.
It moans as she moaned,
pounded and punched
under it before she
took it for her own.
Some nights she's
sure she could run
barefoot thru trees,
bring it back, feed
it milk as if it was
a lost mewling kitten
whose mother had been
killed. Like a bad
child, in its first
home, it was a terror,
threatening and rude.
But when she took
possession everything
changed. Immediately.
It quieted, lost its
hard, rude glow and
trembled, instead of
assaulting. Maybe, she
knows, she's just
dreaming it calls
for her thru dogwood
trees, thru snow. Maybe
if she didn't give

it back she could
have tamed it into
a shy mourning dove

Years Later Lorena Thinks of the Penis She Had for a Day

how, in her hand,
it was so much
less angry,
more like a
scared bird
not the weapon
she'd known
but shrivelling,
scared, a wounded
kitten coiled
into itself, into
her hands as if
she was skin, a
caul it could
find refuge in,
it was no
longer a fist
of blood, punching,
a sword of bone
and because it
seemed to
quiver, dream of
flight she'd
just let it go

CONDOM CHAIN LETTER

use this condom
and then send it on
to the name at the
bottom. You will
be rewarded in
15 days with 11
used safes. Do not
discard. One man did
not believe in this and
a wasp the size of
New England invaded
his house. Now he won't
need more. Your luck
will change soon.
20 condoms won't be
enough for one night:
women will flock to
you as if the tips
were coded with
something they've
felt and need
again. You can't
lose. Put this down
and let your dog eat
it—one man did
and his penis withered
to a thimble of dusty
skin, a feather
crows swooped down
to use for their nest.
That was the last
he saw of it. Send 75

used condoms. Your
hemorrhoids will
disappear. Only your
wallet and your
penis will get bigger.
Another man who threw
this chain letter away lost
everything that extended
more than half an inch
from his body to sharks.
And when he finally
sent it on, fingers and
thighs grew back, his
nose and ear, even a
nub of a penis.
This is no joke.

The Mad Girl Wraps Her Book of Erotica in a Jacket of a Steak Book

She isn't certain about other
riders' eyes, slivering down
past nipples to the words
bulging like a swollen penis
on the page: the woman who finds

the lover who jokes about having a
tail and *does* have one, isn't just
after some, and hooves he rears up to
mount her on with a schlong the size
of a horse, even his balls

all stallion as he plunges
in. She whinnies. The mad girl
wraps their gorging and gulping noises
in what she *hopes* misleads. After
all, in the city, a woman with

The Story of O on her spread knees
might as well be the one with those
lips down there, opening and dripping,
sending up that down there scent.
Safer to look like she was

reading the *Wine Handbook* or
Dr. Rechshaffen's Diet for Life
Time Weight Control, A Better Life.
Only those don't fit and
all that does is *The Steak Book*

with its own back pages of raw

meat dripping, "rare" it says, its spread
of red places damp and glistening,
juices staining the sheet where they're
spread so wildly the mad girl feels

those hanging on subway straps
lean closer, feels their hot breath,
their eyes dilating, panting, getting

wet just imagining plunging into
what, spread before them, they realize
they are starved for

JACKIE-O READS THE STORY OF O AND WONDERS ABOUT HAVING HER OWN PENIS FOR A DAY

If a woman like O, into fashion and
interior design, a woman who wore
only the best Parisian clothes,
knew Ionic columns from Doric ones

could have let such flesh
whales do what they did in every part
of her, mouth, vagina and even
what must have become an incredibly

rash red ass hole. A woman who read
and knew art couldn't be too unlike her.
It's not that she was an environmentalist
out to save some thrashing dying male

manatee or spotted owl and so let
them plunge into the cove of her
skin. She wonders if that's why O put
an owl mask over her head and let her

self be led by a chain? Not that *she* wasn't
led, Jackie sighs. And led on. She might
as well have had a ring filed thru her labia,
been a slave. She's felt branded, had her

own masks, did what she did for love, too,
her hands tied. Like O, her clothes, her
inner feelings and architecture are
her main intrigues. She tries to imagine

herself in O's body. The best way to get
close would be with a penis of her own,

just for a day. She shudders, knows O did
like women too, and her name's even in O's writing,

another pleasure they could share. Her penis
would be like a massive horse between her
legs, that thick warmth that sweeps
her off her feet and won't cheat on

her but let her hips roll with a
deep sensuous pitch, a half ton of snort
and leather after so many years of riding
that giant phallus—often better than,

well, she won't get into *that*. On the night
something starts to grow inside her she whispers
Penis over and over in her breathy soft
way as if to make the word flesh until

skin jolts up, a dick big as an amaryllis,
a favorite flower of O's she's heard, sure to
lure her to a Château in Roissy. "How," Jackie
shivers, "could O, anonymous and cool as me, not be

open to such a stalk." This wouldn't be the first
big O in her life but maybe this time it will stand
for orgasm she pants as she imagines plunging into O
passionately as if she was redecorating the whole

White House. This time she'd have a bone, not
a home of her own, O the sheath she'll fill
as well as she has the others tho this one's
not of black linen or silk but moist as her own mouth.

She'll canter and trot, ride O as she would a stallion.
Afterward, they'll curl in the dark, in a curve as if the shape

230

of the "O" in their names was reflected in their bodies, talk
about other O names, maybe O.J., wish Nicole had *her* own
     penis,

her gun, stick, spear, sword, knife that could if it had to
slice another lap sausage, only they'd use French words,
come up with a barrage as they'd talked about men
who liked to roam. Then they'd go out shopping,

have snails, eager to rush back to that elegant space
with lush interiors to play with, redo a little more
than just the rooms

Jesus Wonders about Going into Partnership with the Mayflower Madam

She knows the tricks, how to
lure and dazzle, soothe aching
hearts with a touch, bring
joy and passion. Not a bad
goal J.C. murmurs, noticing
his followers have gone
or have their own side trips,
hating the homeless,
screaming at whores,
wanting to take food
stamps away from babies.
He knows if the religious
right saw him on the street
they would look at him with
disgust, sure he's a lazy
pan handler, a hippie, a
bum. He sees meanness in
those who wave his name
on a flag, feels more
compassion in the Madam,
more tenderness, more joy.
She takes the time to
please another, gives of her
body and her time unlike
some of the hot dog rabble
rousing righteous guys.
Jesus dials, gets her
answering machine, all
softness and fluttering,
not stones and swords
and guns and he thinks how

together they might teach
something about opening
to joy, about the deepest
communion and what being
entered by the Beloved
really means

OTHER PLACES

AND THESE BONES DO BLOSSOM
(WAR)

WAR

the woman is
amazed not
that the watch
store is
open but that
anyone cares
about the time,
or knows it.
Every part of
her an aide, a
scout sent
out to listen,
to bring back
news to empty
rooms where
people who
hoped it would
be over are
no longer

It Was like Wintergreen

a camouflage
over the babies'
graves. Even as
the Americans
marched in, 2000
were killed. While
the Germans were
surrendering, they
put ivy over the
earth where arms
and legs were
still sticking up.
The Americans
made them rebury
the dead. But the
Germans didn't
put flowers or
memorials over
the prisoners of
war, just left
wintergreen. It
doesn't need light,
it doesn't need
care. You don't have
to think about it

THERE WERE ALWAYS STARS

at night, loud,
exploding the
closeness of
wrinkled silk.
I remember the
smell of my
mother's hair
holding me
curled into her
coolness of
marble and the
hard lines
of a chair
shading us, the
wood becoming
a tree again.
Blue of sky
Trees in the
bottom of a
tea cup. Even
when the one
wall was ash
mother scrubbed
and kept lace
squares on half
the couch, lit
candles. One Friday
bed posts flared
wilder than wax
in silver. It was
all we know, blue
berry jam blue

veins breaking, the
blue of violets,
Nana's blue sweater
one arm shorter,
unravelling.
Shapes dissolve
like margarine
high noon on the
Sahara. Blue the last
color. David's eyes as
the train door shut.
Blue tattoo, blue
flame I'd only
touch once. Every
thing transformed the
way a scalp stuns,
shaved of hair

TREBLINKA

like the sound
of giraffe
necks shattering.
trembling.
Crystal bullets.
I was wrapped
in a blue so
torn and old
it was almost
colorless, blue
of David's eyes
and the light
we could see from
trains. I had
enough of moon
light, hiding
crawling between
barns. Under the
hay my heart was
pounding. Maybe
when they shave
my hair it will
go for a mattress
in Berlin, for
that man I'd
love to spit
at who dreams
of goose fat
sputtering as
he washes his
coarse beard
with soap made

of a sister
you won't know.
If Treblinka was
a color it would
be a hard icy
almost white
blue the color
of flames
they shoved
cribs into. What
shatters becomes
its own blade

SHE SAID I KNOW IT'S ALMOST MIDNIGHT BUT I WANTED TO GIVE YOU THE BARE SKELETON

My father was rich, a Czech. First it was
just the Gipsies. Nobody worried but then
they started liquidating businesses. Mother
looked rich. Jews started having to carry
papers. On a train she saw these young boys
pulling an old man's beard, jabbing his
yamulka. My mother hissed *isn't this*
action beneath you? No one thought she
was a Jew. When they left, she, who mostly
spoke pure German, tried to use the little
Yiddish she knew, but the man on the train
backed away. She was a tough cookie. Had
her kids yanked by Mengele, mother beaten.
Once she had to kneel in a snow bank in a
dress of small pale faded blue flowers.
She came to days later, lived to keep her
sister alive. Each morning friends walked
to the wet ground near the tall electrified
fence, curled near it, couldn't take it.
My mother got them all to turn around, said
she knew they would get out. I was born in
1945 in a tent in Israel, wrapped in a torn
blanket. My mother who never washed a diaper,
never had seen a cow up close turned them
to pets, got pails of milk from one they let
sleep near the bed. At night I heard her
whisper about the camps, how her sister died
the night of liberation in her arms, gasped
it's getting dark then was gone. Mama said
if she'd known what would happen, she would
not have let her suffer so long. There were

snakes in the tent, no food but I didn't know
we were poor. I just thought it was the way
it was, the way once you became a mother, with
breasts and hair down there, blue numbers also
appeared mysteriously, tattooed on your arms

SHE SAID THE GEESE

When she saw them
squabbling over a
crust she started
shivering. But in
the light she felt
the shadows, how
on their knees, in
the camps the young
and old battered wildly
in mud, for the dry
bread. A mouthful
thrown for hundreds,
the smallest,
the frail trampled.
She said the corn
slid thru her
hands. She couldn't
move, toss a crumb.
They weren't geese,
only men and women,
someone dressed in her
sister's clothes,
clawing and scratching
blood and dust

BLACK RAIN, HIROSHIMA

It was as if we
were thrown into
a smelting furnace.
My friend had skin
hanging down like
the meltings of a
candle. Many ran
to the cool of any
water they could
find, hurled them
selves into sewers
or headed for the
River Ota which
soon was thick with
the dead and dying.
Some died on the
river bank, their
heads in the water
having used their
last surge of earthly
energy for a drink

o

Hiromu Morishiti found
her father later that
day lying in a grassy
field. He'd been on
a street car near
downtown, on his
way to work. She
cremated him in

her garden that
night, his eyes
like those grilled
fish. Others slept on
Hijiama Hill, looked
down on the place that
once was their city
lay calling for
mothers, calling
for children calling
for water then not
calling at all

the dripping lilacs, blue petals
battered, holding on, holding
their brightness in hot steamy
air as if to become brighter
once hail melts from the

slick dark stems. A postcard wouldn't
do it. How much should I try to
tell you. If there was a
photograph I'd be the blonde
in the black velvet
fitted suit. It would be Cape
Anne in November. The lilacs would
have flamed and pulled away,

a summer romance
now short as the weeks. The
woman, let's think of her as
a spy, maybe, guerrilla, stealing
into where no one else
could go, camouflaged
as some poet, man-crazed, a
little flaky who visits
rooms she can't stay in,
undresses and lies down with

danger, cocky enough to suppose
she couldn't lose her skin
or her balance. The
blue of lilacs, her
veins thru flesh cashmere,
roadmaps to places where
there are roadblocks.

Even if I was alive,
scars would have
been worn from what
tied me. You take the
lilacs for granted,
the blue leaves in the
bottom of Dresden china,
cyanide glowing with
a blue light that
zaps like no lover

HE'S MOVED EVERYTHING HE NEEDS INTO ONE ROOM

walls of books on
the Holocaust, revolutions
and Nam blocking the
light. Paper from
D-Day, divorce
papers with stains of cups
all over. The velvet
zip bag of medals, part
of the moat around the
mattress he's
curled on under
a brushed cotton quilt:
you couldn't call any
thing in this room
a comforter. Crumbs
from the last three
weeks, machete
in a top drawer, machine
guns, a .44. Librium
crumbled near ashes,
punching bag, the
insides spill out
of like *entrails*
in the jungle he said
I took the man's
intestines, washed them
off in rain water,
stuffed them back into
the slit like
squeezing bread
crumbs into a turkey

In the VA Hospital

You wouldn't believe
the jokes, we were
all glad to get
there and not in a
body bag, at least we
could sing and ogle
blondes, those of us
with eyes still and
lips that could move.
I'd have been out
sooner than 12 months
if it wasn't for the
skin grafts. No one
felt funny because
nobody had everything
they'd been born with.
Even the quadriplegics
would go on about girls.
Even in the copters
with blood filling the
cockpit, matting
hair, the first thing
those who could talk
whimpered or moaned
was, "Hey, mate, do I
still have my balls?"

Hearing of Reagan's Trip to Bitburg

as new leaves turn
the size of babies'
hands, the last
thing mothers saw
as the screaming
wriggling bodies were
thrown in fires, hands
buried above some grave
as if waving goodby
or pulling you with
them. Suddenly I'm
back in the yellow
room, color of willows,
sun tulips, daffodils
breaking down. Woke
up each night dreaming
of tunnels and fire,
the words whispered in
front of the apartment,
rain of the blue
tattoos. The gas,
words like *cattle car*
changed as the word
camp, so when I went
to Camp Hochelago I
waited for gas, held
my breath, couldn't
sleep with lights off

IF HAIR COULD SIFT DOWN

make a silt soft as the
three feet of rose petals
Cleopatra had surrounding
her bed, a swamp for lovers to

open in or a lake of soft
rose leaves, the sheets on the bed
would float in the musk waves.
Hair shaved, leaving the women in line

whimpering. *For cleanliness is
next to* signs said. Nobody
didn't want to believe tho
the air was strange smoke.

If braids chopped from a young girl
days before she'll even bleed, herded
over stone, her mother singing
Hatikvah could drift back, hang

on trees like Spanish moss
or float onto a snow field out
from mattresses and pillows they
were shoved into for years in a

Gestapo son's wife's closet,
if they could yank free as the
skull it once hugged couldn't,
except in a last breath in fire,

a bird might pluck what didn't go
cinders, what escaped in a

rough officer's hand before the head
was left in the square on a stick

for warning, an eye sliding down
to mud. Fifty years later, what
cushioned the lips pressing a young girl
in an attic they hid in and warmed,

brushed 200 times by the light of a candle
might be woven into a nest in dark
pines, make a cove feathers would
uncoil in, fragile and as wild to fly

as what the hair once held

BLACK TRILLIUM AND APRICOT WIND
(PLACE)

North of Cottonwood

rose lichen
   gamble oak
       globe mallow

bent in rain

blue lupine

juniper mistletoe

it rains and keeps raining

these rocks
       pulled from each other

two million years ago

wrenched like a woman
whose child is grabbed

on a cattle car

smashed into stone

her eyes, streaked
       like tonight's sky

a Monday, all *sipapu,*

a spirit entrance

into the underworld

ENCHANTED MESA

2 small babies
held in dryness.
They found these
mummies in a
limestone cave
born in New Mexico
around the time
of Beowulf. One's
buried on a cradle
board of peeled
twigs, straps
hold the body
in a cocoon of
yucca and cotton
and small ears of
corn. 3 pieces of
pottery as a burial
offering. The blue
clay jars bigger
than the baby

o

The other new
born infant
buried without a
cradle, wrapped
in cotton cloth
and turkey feathers.
The robe tied on
with 3 strips of
yucca. Most of the

robe feathers
eaten by insects.
Only the quills left.
A matting of split
willow covers
the wrapped baby
who was buried
beneath the
floor of the
mother's house
with the hope
that the spirit
might be reborn,
come back to her
in the flesh again

THIRTY MILES WEST OF CHICAGO

paint chips slowly.
It's so still you
can almost hear it
pull from a porch.

Cold grass claws
like fingers in a
wolf moon. A man
stands in corn bristles

listening, watching
as if something
could grow from
putting a dead child

in the ground

Things that Shine in Quebec City as the Sun Falls

light on the ball
of glass, on
the puddles
under the Hilton.
The St Lawrence glows,
the flag poles,
edges of buildings.
A yellow car in the
salmon light.
Lights are starting to go on.
Green copper roofs glow,
shadows of clouds
over sailboats
on the water.
The smell of leaves,
cool wind blowing.
The water
a ripple of light
like a flag of glass.
Diamond ripples.
I think of Diamond Head,
light that seemed
magical in a strange
town. The only
familiar sign is
one that says
Kresge's. Light
that will glow
when what
seems to
might not.
Green diamonds,

red diamonds,
blue diamonds
starting to cover
the hill

New Hampshire

wild cat in the
wood pile, deer

you can't see
I drift with

the poem you
sent into an

underground
river where

Indians eat
fish so old

they have no
eyes. If I

shut my eyes
I hear the

water that
flows under

the columbine
When I touch

the chair I hear
bluebirds that

were wild in its
leaves when there

were red flowers
in its branches

MIDDLEBURY POEM

Milky summer nights,
the men stay waiting, First National Corner
where the traffic light used to be, wait

as they have all June evenings of their lives.
Lilac moss and lily of the valley
sprout in the cooling air as

Miss Damon, never late for thirty years,
hurries to unlock the library, still
hoping for a sudden man to spring tall from the

locked dark of mysterious card catalogues, to
come brightening her long dusty shelves.
And halfway to dark

boys with vacation bicycles
whistle flat stones over the bridge,
longing for secret places where
rocks are blossoming girls with damp thighs.

Then nine o'clock falls thick on lonely books
and all the unclaimed fingers and
as men move home through bluemetal light,
the Congregational Church bells

ringing as always four minutes late,
the first hayload of summer rumbles through
town and all the people shut their eyes
dreaming a wish

Black roses, flattened
bougainvillaea. Cappuccino,
baguettes of bread. Sun,
like a purple iceplant of
light sucked behind
Berkeley Hills.
Sidewalk vendors
pick up glass beads,
copper. One smooths
a shirt lime and
blood is already faded
on. Rice in pots for
men in long overcoats
you know they've slept
in. A thin dazed woman
in white cotton could
be heading for a safari,
arms blotched, tattooed,
all tracks. Night's
thick as soupy rice
a young girl passes
out on corners. A gold
capped tooth glows
from an alley. Hashish,
tomato soup and vomit
slither over a man's tweed
coat that has the shape of
his bones. He crosses the
street with a shopping cart
piled with geography books,
maps, quilts some patches
are missing from as if

the holes were windows to
new shores he and his cat
look toward. The cat
regal on neatly folded
rags that in this light
could be a silk and
velvet throne, its leash
rhine stone studded. Both,
maybe, heading toward a beach
of palms and coconut leaves
only sun and surf lick
perhaps in Maui if
the cart floats

THE MAN COMING OUT OF DARKNESS

as sky lets go
of kohl. Silver
foam lace, lemon
curd sand. He

walks out of
fog whitely green
as the sweater
marked "sea mist."

Sea weed hair,
wrists drip eels.
Koa thighs, fingers.
Palms fling their

fonds and the
longhaired Japanese
girls whose foot
prints the sea's

already licking
take him, hold
him for as long
as they want him

with their Nikons

WILD HORSES DYING

After the fourth day
they stand and sway
like a weight on
a rope that
moves when nothing
seems to move it
They fall against
each other,
crumbling stones

They are so light
the wind moves them
They could be water

hooves and hair
in the rippled sand
like shells

AFTERWARD

First we burned even
the birch covered with
punky mushrooms, the
dried pearwood, cherry
then wrapped in electric
blankets when houses
still had light. Later
we dressed in four
layers of wool. Suddenly
see thru nylon silk, those
sheer blouses young girls
saved for, were useless
as transparent bikini
tops to a woman with
both breasts freshly
gone. It was strange
to be glad for drawers
of my dead husband's
sweaters, the youngest
wore them as a dress
when she still could walk

o

Televisions sets can't,
like dressers drawers,
be used for the smallest
coffins. With the trees
turning into hulks of
driftwood, squirrels
gnaw thru pebbles in
the roof. Grass stays

grey into what should
be summer. Those left
shiver in houses where
there's nothing left to
burn. A woman washing
her babies notices blood
in the sink, that the
child's hair tangles
around her ankles and
wrists like sea weed
or rope as candles
sputter, fall in
to themselves too

o

Cars that used to sound
like the sea even thru the
ring of maples are suddenly
still. For days people waited
for phones to work, for
something to come thru the
snow on tv on channels as
unlike what they'd seen
as faces of those survivors
at Nagasaki. It took days
to see how what we couldn't
see was turning the grass
and leaves colorless as
petals pressed in a book.
Instead of cars, within
the month, we began to
hear digging. Women who
didn't know how roots
tangled under houses

had to dig graves. It
was like they were
scooping out parts of
themselves the way they'd
scooped out a squash and
stuffed it with croutons
and celery for Thanksgiving
to bury babies they'd held
weeks before, thankful
there was no direct hit
only to watch them roll
into a ball and turn
still as the branches.
Soon all the lawns
were mud

o

phones die first, tv
channels turn snow. But
no spoons or bones melt
into hair or smoldering
ashes. Doctors disagree
about rads. Sun still
turns copper roofs
cherry but a young
boy says the milk
tastes odd. A 12 year
old girl's hair falls
out overnight, a baby
turns from a nipple
weeks before there's
no oil or gas and a
child is buried in
dust of a favorite

trunk as mothers
touch their children
like women clutching
what was nearly torn
from them, stroke
skin and lips, stunned
at how what seemed
ordinary now dazzles

THIS LONG WINTER

with the pipes freezing
rust on the walls like
blood and the dog that
got out of the fenced
in yard put to sleep
in 3 hours. There's
ice in the toilet

plaster in the bread
and then no bread
The hot water tank
breaks but doesn't
drown the itch mites
Ice shoves the birds
away, by February
there's no dope
Under the snow the
canoe is dissolving

It's easier when the
darkest snow wraps
the house in wind and
you can't see thru
the plastic, days
all we can do is
curl up in a quilt
and listen to the
maple on the pebble
roof push what is in
to a puff of breath
that drifts into
the wild apples,
try to get warm

272

Dark Matter May Bind the Universe

enigmatic material
that gives off no
light, no radiation

may keep what it
seems could fly off,
galaxy clusters,

other cosmic clumps,
from flying apart,
there, like what

you can't put your
fingers on in someone
who's lost everything

but doesn't whirl
herself into
chaos, dark matter,

a shadowy appearance
like a spider being
pressed against a

huge invisible wall,
images of something
embedded, a cloud

that would have
dissipated unless it
was held in darkness

HERE

something as mysterious
as quarks, a pull like
naked charm sets in,
changes the air.
Mysterious as what
happens in houses
where women who live
together a long time
begin to get their
period on the same
day. Something un-
spoken runs from
pillow to pillow
while we sleep
like mice in the wall
from the field of
apples and elderberry
into a sea of glazed
green reflecting
more colors than an
ordinary prism. Then
the birds come, you
drift all day in and
out of yourself,
fly until a car churns
up thru the gravel
like lights coming on
at the end of the
movie

VIOLET JELLY

picking the leaves
Monday early in
a cool rain huddled
in wet sweatshirts
Hours in the grey
knees and fingers
numb, our skin
smells of violets
while they soak
in the red pan
overnight till we
boil them down
licking the green
Then the pectin
turns them lilac
We pour them into
glass, amethyst
the sun comes thru
on the window
after snow

WILD THYME

all the way down the
sloped hill under
the white pines
You should pick it when
the sun is low and night's
water is wild on the
red grass. Don't kick up
the sweet lace, twist
or crunch out the smell
But pick it while it's
sucking up afternoon
light, its smell on
your fingers like
a lover, pin it to
beams in rooms apricot
light will sneak thru
glazing bare walnuts,
knowing the leaves
still wait in snow
full of what drew
you to it

THAW

Ice comes undone
Skin shining and
hair full of
March

women spill out of
offices their
bones whispering

Glazed orchards
and vines coming back
Green is under the
snow the women's

arms seem to open
as if to lift them past
fluorescent air
toward whatever

mysteries
are hidden from them
Later nearly
blinded by water and

light they'll move
a 1 o'clock wave
their hair folding
back into

rooms of
machines and paper. But

no desks can
hold such

dreaming blood,
drunk on the poems
sun makes
in their bodies

Printed July 1997 in Santa Barbara
& Ann Arbor for the Black Sparrow Press by
Mackintosh Typography & Edwards Brothers Inc.
Text set in Calisto by Words Worth.
Design by Barbara Martin.
This first edition is published in paper wrappers;
there are 200 hardcover trade copies;
100 hardcover copies have been numbered &
signed by the author; & 20 copies lettered A–T
with an original artwork by Lyn Lifshin
have been handbound in boards by
Earle Gray & are signed by the poet.

LYN LIFSHIN has written more than 90 books and chapbooks of poetry, most recently *Blue Tattoo*, poems of the Holocaust published by Event Horizon, and *Marilyn Monroe*, a collection of poems published by Quiet Lion Press. Her works appear widely in magazines and anthologies. She has edited four major anthologies of women's writing: *Tangled Vines*, a collection of mother and daughter poems first published by Beacon Press and then reprinted in an expanded edition by Harcourt, Brace Jovanovich, *Ariadne's Thread*, a collection of women's diaries and journals published by Harper and Row and *Lips Unsealed*, a collection of women's confidences. She gives workshops in connection with these collections as well as writing and publishing workshops and workshops using particular subjects to stimulate writing: mirrors, feelings about war, writing through the American urban landscape, writing from the inside out and the outside in and sensuality and sexuality for women.

She is the subject of an award-winning documentary film, *Not Made of Glass*, by Mary Ann Lynch distributed by Women Make Movies along with a collection of poems by the same name distributed by Karista Press. She has won many grants and fellowships including a New York State Caps Grant, a Bread Loaf Scholarship and a Jack Kerouac Award and spends her time between upstate New York and a goose pond in Virginia. *Cold Comfort* (1997) is her first book from Black Sparrow Press.